W9-CEA-089

Mum's the Word

The Wit and Wisdom of a Semi-Sweet Grandmother

Evelyn Abrahams

Published by HPBooks®
P.O. Box 5367
Tucson, AZ 85703
ISBN: 0-89586-401-0
Library of Congress Catalog Card Number: 84-62855
©1985 HPBooks, Inc.
Printed in U.S.A.
1st Printing

Publisher:
Rick Bailey

Editorial Director:
Randy Summerlin

Editor:
Jacqueline Sharkey

Art Director:
Don Burton

Typography:
Cindy Coatsworth, Michelle Claridge

Book Manufacture:
Anthony B. Narducci

Illustrator:
Don Berry

Cover Photograph:
Hazel Burton

In Dedication

With love to Edna Hirshberg,
my mother, my inspiration.

Acknowledgments

I wish to express my gratitude to the editors of HPBooks for their excellence in preparing the manuscript for publication; to the HPBooks staff for its enthusiasm and faith in my work; and to Linda Johns and Anne Ready who carried me across the tides of media.

I am greatly indebted to the women with whom I laughed, cried and shared the drama of grandmotherly realities. They are the book.

The devotion and love of my grandmothers are the precious golden threads that bind the memories of my childhood.

Special appreciation goes to my dear friends who offered excellent suggestions and stimulated many of the thoughts expressed in these chapters. Thanks to my aunts Anna and Jean who recruited many grandmothers.

I wish to express special tribute to the late Judith Finke whose gentle wisdom and humor helped me in the early drafts of the manuscript.

Last, and with much love, I thank my husband for his valuable suggestions and sensitive counsel, and for being my best critic.

Contents

Foreword

Mum's the Word puts the spotlight on the experiences of grandmothers. It is also a quiet, introspective look at the family and the intensely personal ways in which we affect one another's lives.

Whether stoic, saint or culprit, every grandmother is a character worthy of an author, if only because she loves her grandchildren "no matter what." Grandmotherhood brings out a mother's character in profound ways.

Grandmotherhood is a timeless and intriguing topic. Being a grandmother has never made any woman famous, but numerous famous women have been and are grandmothers.

In *Mum's the Word*, we meet many women and their families. These women reveal with extraordinary candor treasured moments, longings and the ironies of family relationships. As they reflect upon their experiences, we may find their lives touch our own.

Most females are destined to be wives, mothers, mothers-in-law and grandmothers. With luck, some will become great-grandmothers. Their lives cover a span of time and range of experience that enable them to understand the crosscurrents buffeting a family at different times.

Mum's the Word is based on interviews, observations, conversations, correspondence, friendships, my own grandmotherhood and many years of practice as a psychotherapist. It is a sincere tribute to grandmothers everywhere, and is intended to bring happiness and convey messages that might help to make this world a better and happier place.

Evelyn Abrahams

1
About Grandmothers . . .

Grandmothers come in different shapes, sizes, colors and ages. To be a grandmother one must be a woman. But one must also be a person with the courage and personality to survive emotional hardships. One is not necessarily born to the task.

Some women say being a grandmother is overrated, and some say the same thing about motherhood. But why argue? Grand-motherhood is what it is—for some a privilege, for others a predicament. Many women become totally involved in the experience, but some seem to travel through grandmotherhood like tourists.

Women do not plan or choose to become grandmothers. They are not consulted. They do not supervise the production. Grand-children arrive. It's as simple as that. There are grandmothers whose blood does not course in the veins of their grandchildren, but who get the title through marriage or adoption. They are among the most loved.

In the universal scheme of things, the grandmother's role may be insignificant. But in her own little world, it can be tremendously important. The grandmother makes an indelible imprint on family life, passing on traditions and establishing family bonds. The extent of a grandmother's role is dictated by her personal choices and by circumstances. No two grandmothers are alike. Children think this is advantageous. They feel fortunate if their grannies are different.

During the past several decades, many people cast aside numerous rules of conduct. Now these people are turning back toward traditional values. This may explain why grandmothers are getting more attention these days. They are being called back from retirement to active duty. And they gladly answer the call. A grandmother is never too tired to help her family cope with a crisis of faith or trust. Advances in medicine and spare parts have extended grandma's endurance. How else could she come to grips with the changing realities of modern living before becoming a period piece?

There are at least a hundred reasons why grandmothers are extolled in songs and paintings, and honored in some nations with a national holiday. Despite cultural differences, they have similar roles everywhere. Whether they are rich or struggling to make ends meet, they have much in common. Their virtues include dependability and availability. Grandmothers are so competent that when they settle on the moon someday, they will tidy up the place and redecorate it.

Grandmothers long to share specific thoughts and feelings arising from their personal experiences. For example, they might want to discuss how they feel about always being seated next to the difficult or unimportant people at weddings and other family affairs. They might want to express how they feel about being ignored and invisible. They might want to talk about what being a grandmother means to them at a particular moment in time.

One issue many grandmothers want to discuss is "mom-blaming." Grandmothers are tired of being blamed for all their children's problems. They don't appreciate being lectured about what they did improperly or ineptly way back when. They admit to having bungled here and there, but grandmothers grow up, too. They are refusing to take the blame for their children's phobias, bossiness, laziness, inability to "establish enduring relationships" (as therapists put it) or "failure to achieve full orgasmic potential."

Another issue grandmothers would like to discuss is how to answer the troublesome question, "What should we do about Grandma?" Grandmothers have differing views on how to resolve this problem!

And there is one other situation grandmothers would like to talk about. This involves their struggle to continue alone, without a partner. They often yearn to share their loneliness and tears with a loved one.

Some authors who write about grandmothers believe that they know and understand the difficulties and rewards. But their stories often are untrue, misleading, woven from hearsay. Grandmothers are their own best biographers. When they speak about their lives, it's worth listening to what they have to say, even if they embroider it a little.

Grandmothers seem to agree on several issues. They believe that grandmothers must have a sense of humor to be successful; that they must be prepared for the unexpected; that being a grandmother is easier than being a mother; that loving their grandchildren is natural; and that enjoying their grandchildren is a blessing.

Not all women are eager to become grandmothers. Some have barely finished groping through parenthood and don't want to assume new responsibilities. They have their own plans.

Other women can't wait for the begetting to begin. They are anticipating the event while their son or daughter is tying the knot. The thought spreads like warm sunshine through their bones.

Young grandmothers usually have several advantages. They tend to have more imagination. They are closer to their own childhoods than older grandmothers. Their worlds are still expanding, too. But there is much to be said for older grandmothers. After all, it isn't their fault that young couples are postponing having children while they concentrate on careers or long-term adventures between the percales.

This situation changes when young women realize their biological clocks are running out. Then they lend an ear to Mum's plea: "When will you begin populating the world and make me a grandmother?" More and more frequently the answer is: "OK, Mum, you win. What's your preference—boy, girl or twins?"

This is why ladies in their 60s and 70s are becoming grandmothers for the first time. They may be too old for a skateboard and too young for a cane, but they are just the right age to push a stroller in the park.

2
In the Beginning

So, you've just become a grandmother! Congratulations! It is your moment in the sun, and you should be treated like a prima donna.

Life turns full circle when our children become parents. Hearts flutter in gratitude and wonder. When a daughter or son hands us the baby for the first time, there is pride, joy and expectancy in his or her eyes. A rush of tenderness flows through us and the new parents. Everyone's eyes get misty. We are aware of experiencing something for the first time. The link between the generations is forged and love overwhelms us.

How do we find words? We don't. The words find us. Some women regard grandmotherhood as a revitalizing experience, an opportunity to learn more about life and about themselves. Others decide not to get too involved in grandmotherhood.

Almost every woman can describe in detail the events surrounding the birth of her first child. Later in life, she also remembers in detail the arrival of her first grandchild:

It was 4 o'clock in the morning when the phone rang with the good news that we were grandparents. It was no ordinary day. I am a grandmother! Such complex emotions! I wasn't sure what to do next. I was overwhelmed. I felt different and yet the same.

I was certain about one thing, however. I was ready for grandmotherly questions! Was the baby born by natural childbirth? How much does it weigh? Is it a boy or girl? What's the baby's name? Ask! Ask!

Sally P.

My first grandchild was born soon after I fell asleep, exhausted. I had sat up all night with my daughter while she tried to make up her mind whether she was in labor. My un-blinking eyes had been glued on her face and enlarged abdomen. Then I missed all the action (thank heaven). My daughter and her husband had been thoroughly rehearsed in the Lamaze natural childbirth method. They also insisted on training me as understudy in case my son-in-law was not available at the crucial moment.

But he had vowed to be there. Not to worry, he assured me. Wild dogs could not keep him from his wife's side. Indeed they didn't. Yet my daughter had neither husband nor mother with her at the moment of truth. I was asleep on the sofa. Her husband was on the hospital floor, where he had fainted.

We should have known this would happen. Charlie always had turned green near hospitals. As my daughter pushed through the final labor pain, she took a look at her husband and shrieked, "Doc, forget the method! Bring on the dope . . . and take care of Charlie!"

16

*That is how our Daniel entered the world. And that is how
I came through my first grandmotherly test.*

Lois D.

Lamaze and other natural childbirth methods have become extremely popular. Everyone benefits from Lamaze, except the grandmother-to-be. The system has overlooked her. She waits nervously for the baby to be born. She is ready to help in any way—by providing transportation, comfort (pillows in the car), something tasty to eat to take the mind off labor pains. She has been unable to sleep for weeks. She looks forward to enjoying her transition from mum to granny.

"During the last months of my daughter's pregnancy, like most mums I worried that something might go wrong," Elizabeth said. "If I could have worn amulets against the various possibilities I conjured up in my mind, I would have done so.

"From mum to grandma is easy. It's the suspense that isn't. I was put on notice when 'the water broke' just as I was filling the refrigerator for the homecoming celebration—whenever it would be. Little did I know that I was to have only an overnight respite.

"Mummy, baby and daddy 'roomed in' for 24 hours, then returned home as a family. I never had a chance to get my hair done. I never left the house. Yes, the Lamaze system overlooked Grandma."

But love is energizing. Grandma will be standing at the door poised for action when the trio arrives, and that is exactly where they want her to be. As the baby is placed in grandma's waiting arms, the new parents beam. "Hey, this is your Granny. Say hello."

I was just a mother and mother-in-law. Then within 48 hours I had two grandchildren. My daughter and daughter-in-law had their babies in two different towns. I was dashing between two hospitals, lugging two potted chrysanthemums and two life-sized teddy bears. Where did I get the strength? The bustle, excitement and joy kept me going.

Cynthia N.

The first look at the baby follows a traditional pattern. We are filled with relief, reverence, anticipation. We are on the brink of a precious new experience, and we can hardly wait.

But hospitals have strict rules about newborns. Even though you can hear the babies through the nursery wall, you can see them only at specific hours. No amount of pleading or political influence will get you a preview. You have to wait until curtain time.

Grandparents, fathers, relatives and close friends wait before the hallowed window. Finally, the curtain parts to reveal rows of small cribs on wheels, each containing an infant. For a moment—only a moment—they all look alike, swathed in white diapers. Eager faces press against the glass. Eyes quickly search the room, as if we could choose the baby we like best. Then we focus a proprietary eye on one particular crib and recognize that baby as "ours."

To grandpa, all the infants may "look like little monkeys." To grandma, each child is a miracle. As she gazes at the babies, she smiles beatifically. She is acutely aware of her emotions. She thinks:

> Thank God! (It's over.)
> So *that* one is *ours.* (She puts on her glasses.)
> He's so *red!* (It will fade.)
> Definitely favors our side of the family. (Uncle Louie.)
> All that *hair!* (Full-term pregnancy.)
> Do I *look* like a grandmother? (Yes and no.)
> Why am I crying? (Overwhelmed. Can't explain.)
> Are they *sure* that one is ours? (The wristband is the guarantee, but mistakes happen.)
> Does this mean I'm getting *old?* (Hmmm.)

I still remember how silly I was and how I didn't give a hoot while cooing and waving at the babies with the other grandmothers. I still remember wondering whether the whole world was asleep and whether I should wake everyone up to tell them, "I am a grandmother!" What other experience could inspire so much sentimental insanity?

Beatrice H.

The baby is doing nothing, doesn't even know I exist, and already is making me very, very happy. I can hardly wait to hold my grandchild in my arms.

Tessie B.

I wasn't exactly thrilled with my daughter's choice of a husband. His mother was not exactly thrilled that my daughter wasn't pregnant after a year. However, a few sessions with the fertility clinic solved the problem. My daughter was obviously very pregnant. The son-in-law who seemed so pathetic and inept became the father of triplets. All boys, no less! Overnight he became a big organizer, Mr. Efficiency. He gave us lists and sent us out for more diapers, blankets, bottles, you name it. We grandmothers did it and loved it. He chose the cribs and carriage and convertible highchair tables. We gladly paid. His mother kept no record of who paid for what and neither did I. The triplets cemented our friendship.

Florence P.

23

I set up a trust fund for my first grandchild's education at Harvard the day he arrived. As I held my infant grandson in my arms and looked at his beautiful long fingers encircling one of mine, I said, "Buster, make up your mind to practice, because you have the hands of a violinist. You will have the best teachers. I already know who to contact when the time comes. Maybe we should insure your hands."

Sylvia R.

My first grandchild had more pictures taken of him during his first month of life than any of the later grandchildren had. He was given more presents and got to more places than the others. Everything he wore was brand new and monogrammed. The others had to take what they got.

Irene L.

For me, suddenly having a grandchild to love opened a wellspring that flowed inward, filling spaces I didn't know were there and waiting.

Jan P.

When I first saw my grandchild, I cringed inside. The baby had long black hair low on her forehead and down her arms. The kind of face that would move people to say, "What a healthy-looking child!" I could hardly meet my daughter's eyes as I said, "She is a beauty." My daughter answered, "I'm glad you think so, too, Mom. She really is gorgeous." You should see that dimpled heartbreaker now! And talented? Don't ask.

Rona B.

My first grandchild: Those first two months were unforgettable. Friends phoned and gave luncheons and teas in honor of my new status. They "oohed" and "ahhed" over the photographs taken in the hospital. Little did I know that soon I would be expected to respond similarly with every grandchild they had—the same luncheons, same menus, same charming little gifts, same picture routine, same questions-and-answers game.

Maria F.

Naming the Baby

This may present problems. Secretly, we hope they'll name the baby after one of us or in memory of someone we love. We may want grandpa's name (Mortimer) carried on. We'll be lucky if they use an *M*.

There are other considerations, too. If the baby is named for someone on one side of the family, what about the other side? And what about the name itself? What child wants to be called "Junior," "Little Eddie" or "Julius" all his life?

Terry, Leslie, Ronnie, Toni and Sandy are names that cause trouble. It begins when presents come in pink instead of blue. The confusion doesn't end until the child becomes old enough to change his or her name.

Giving a baby two first names also causes confusion. One is enough to remember. Charles Augustus surely will prefer "Charlie." Daniel Sean probably will opt for Dan. Nan Laurie, Mary Jane, Sara Lee and Lillie May will have a more difficult choice to make.

Nicknames also cause problems. Babies grow into people. The preemie everyone calls "tiny Tim" may become a weight lifter. At age 40, April may not find her nickname as cute as it was at age 12.

We can tell our children what we think about names. After all, grandparents have some natural rights! But parents have the right to make the final choice about names. After all, it's *their* baby!

A grandmother may believe that a name is a lifelong statement. Even so, she will try not to be upset when the baby isn't called *Helen*, after her mother, but *Allegra*, after her son-in-law's cousin. She consoles herself with the thought that the baby is healthy and has all 10 fingers and 10 toes. What's in a name, anyway? It's too early in the game to sulk. So grandmother makes a quiet retreat and tries to be vaguely polite about the name. She remembers that the system simply doesn't allow her to affect any major decisions at this point.

The Grandmother Trap

We think we're *indispensable*. Every call for help means, "Drop everything and run!"

We are the experts. Who can do it better?

We feel so obligated. Our own needs come last.

We are martyrs. We eat fast food when we visit our grandchildren and pretend we've always loved it.

We dream of escaping, taking a trip to China, joining the women's movement, learning transcendental meditation. Instead, we take another trip to the zoo and then spend the evening reading Dr. Seuss without skipping a line.

What's happening? The Grandmother Trap!

We are on vacation. We feel relaxed and carefree. Suddenly, the print on the pages of the book we are reading disappears and we see the face of our grandchild. We are overcome by how much we miss the baby. We notify the management we are leaving in the morning and call the family to tell them we'll be home sooner than expected.

We burst into tears when we get back and the baby is wearing a little white shirt emblazoned, *I LOVE GRANDMA.*

We can't refuse the child anything. The parents know we will never neglect the little one .

We love to see the child enjoying the food we've prepared. But how we suffer when the baby throws up after overeating!

We never complain when we are in the bathtub, surrounded by toy duckies, plastic gurgling bottles and tiny boats turning upside down, and our grandchild insists on washing our back one more time.

We don't mind standing on our feet for hours to be sure our grandchild is the first in line for tickets and gets the best spot to view the parade.

We develop a reputation in the family for getting things done. We even believe it when they say, "Grandma, c'mon, do it! You do it the best."

That's the Grandmother Trap.

Maybe we like it. Maybe we don't. But we feel like traitors when we say "no." We lose our best friend — ourselves.

Maybe we just aren't cut out to be "Supergrandmothers." If we aren't, let's admit it and fill the role our own way.

I wish I could grow a third arm. Can you imagine trying to go to the bathroom with one child over my shoulder and the other clinging to my skirt? Neither one wants to let go of me. What I need is a grandmother's helper. How did I manage this with my own children? I know. It's what I wanted then and what I want now. It's my cage, and it's filled with everything I love. It will be a sad day when I leave it. I don't want to get out. Ever!!

Jeanette B.

"This is what I've been waiting for," Harriet said. She was smiling and showing some new fatigue wrinkles. "My daughter had three children in 28 months. Her husband is studying for a degree. I'm at their apartment whenever I can be to pitch in. There's so much to do. I love it. It's fun! Nothing gives me greater pleasure. The grandchildren are absolutely adorable, with the same blue eyes and yellow curls, as if they had been cloned. No matter what I do, it's not enough. I'm completely exhausted, but I don't mind. My husband says that sometimes I look almost comatose. Maybe I have a problem?

Harriet G.

Some mums know how they got into the Grandmother Trap, but they don't know how to get out. They need a psychological map.

Grandma's feet are killing her, she's light-headed from martyrdom, her back has given out and a casserole is in the oven. She knows her friends are playing bridge. With a faint smile bravely in place, she secretly plans ways to slide out of the Grandmother Trap.

What's going on in my life, anyway? I really need to talk this over with someone besides myself. You see, my son was on an assignment in South America. But this was the first grandchild in the family, so what difference did it make if the baby was 10,000 miles away in South America or next door? I'll tell you.

I got on an airplane and went. It cost a small fortune. I arrived like an official taking over the day after my granddaughter was born and got on my son and daughter-in-law's nerves right away. They had household help, but in my opinion it was poor quality. I knew what had to be done. I cleaned the house. I cooked. I trained a schoolgirl who spoke some English. It was all very hard work.

My daughter-in-law was suffering. She couldn't sit because she had stitches. In a strange city and in a foreign language, I found a rubber ring for her to sit on. I taught her the little things I had learned from my mother, such as how to nurse a baby while lying down.

"It's so good to have a mom around who knows how to be a real grandmother," my daughter-in-law said. "Don't leave yet. I need you."

It was a dangerous moment. I smiled, kissed her, the baby and my son, and packed my valise.

Kiki R.

Only a grandmother constructs a Grandmother Trap. She leaps into it with a full heart, willing hands, eyes shining with grandmotherly zeal. Does she hesitate? Weigh the pros and cons of canceling previous plans or appointments? Not on your life! That's the Grandmother Trap, and she has two extra keys just in case.

Scott Waits for His Grandmother
(A short, short story)

As a grandmother, I'm not usually called upon to baby-sit. But when my daughter asked me to fetch my 6-year-old grandson from school, that was different. It was the perfect day to relax and take an afternoon nap—rainy, windy, a cold winter sky. Just what I needed to settle down in my warm house with a drink and a good book. But this was not to be.

My daughter gave me clear instructions: "Meet Scott at precisely 3 p.m. and Mommy, please don't be late or Scotty will be standing in the rain." I listened carefully. "You know he's just over a bad cold," she continued. "Take him straight to the car and don't let him dawdle in puddles. You know how he loves to splash around."

I nodded reassuringly. "Not to worry, dear," I said. "I'll bring him home safe, sound and dry."

"You can't miss him," she said. "He's wearing the red boots you gave him and his yellow raincoat and rain hat. Be sure he doesn't forget his Mickey Mouse lunch box in the classroom. If he does forget, it won't hurt to take him back into the building and see that he gets it. He must learn to take care of his things."

Wrinkling her brow, she paused, looking at me dubiously. As an afterthought, she said, "Get there before 3, Mommy. In this weather, parents get there early to park their car closer to the gate." She took a deep breath. "That's about it. Scotty knows you'll be meeting him, and he'll be looking out for you. Enjoy each other. It's so good to have a dependable mom. I love you." She hugged me and left.

I arrived at the school at 2:45 sharp. I couldn't get near the school gate. Cars were already double-parked, and parents were seated behind the wheel reading and waiting. I settled for a place a block away. What the hell, I thought, I'll get out and walk to the entrance. That way, Scott will see me as soon as he comes through.

It was really a miserable, wet day. Too bad I hadn't worn my raincoat, but at least there was an umbrella in the car. I opened it and walked toward the entrance, my eyes fastened on the familiar green door that the first- and second-graders came out of. Cold drops of rain slid off the umbrella and down my neck as I continued to peer at the door, straining my neck so I wouldn't miss my Scotty. Hmmm, what if they let the little ones out early because of the weather? I stood in a gray curtain of rain watching the school door as if my life depended on it.

My shoes were filling with water and my socks were soaking wet. Never mind. Any minute now. I tried to bolster my confidence and stamina. The green door was opening, children were pouring out. I struggled with a feeling of terror. Almost every child coming through that door was wearing a yellow raincoat with a matching hat and red boots, and was carrying a Mickey Mouse lunch box.

39

I began to pray. Dear God, please help me. God has a kindly concern for little children. All I was asked to do was simply to bring my grandson home, and I can't even recognize him. Is it possible a mature woman can panic so easily? I thought age and experience never let a woman down. Whoever said it was easy to be a grandmother?

The daymares began. My imaginative wings were beating wildly. Poor little Scott, frightened, looking for his grandmother, feeling so alone and abandoned. I could see the tears running down his cheeks, mixing with the rain and probably a runny nose. Poor child, thinking he'd been forgotten—no one there to meet him and take him home.

At that moment, I wanted to kill myself. I will, I thought, if anything has happened to that child. What a failure as a grandmother I have turned out to be. I can't even identify my own grandson. Then I began to get angry. "Damn it, Scott, where the heck can you be?" Every time another yellow-raincoated kid appeared, my heart leaped. Good God, can a grandmother fail to know her own flesh and blood? Yes!

3:15. No Scott. A few stragglers were still coming through the green door. The rain had thoroughly penetrated my shoes, and the wind made it difficult to hold on to the umbrella. Should I inquire at the office? But what if I missed him while I was inquiring? How could I be in two places at the same time? Better wait. Pray some more.

The rain was coming down heavily. Suddenly, I had an

idea. The police! THAT was a possibility! What would I tell them? Child missing? Oh no! I couldn't handle that.

The green door closed with finality. There wasn't a child left in the schoolyard. He's been kidnapped! I started to gasp for air. Panic. Anxiety began triggering an asthma attack.

I began talking to myself out loud. These things can only happen to others, never to us. How could I face my daughter? My heart was pounding. Better get back to the car and think it through before my imagination went wild.

Back at the car at last. I stopped dead in my tracks. I couldn't believe my eyes. There was Scott standing in a puddle, quite unconcerned. Thank you, Father in heaven. You saved my credibility as a grandmother.

I gathered my grandson into my soggy arms, held him close and felt the water sliding down his raincoat under my shirt and up my coat sleeves. I glanced at my feet in the puddle. I felt like the survivor of a flood, and thought I might be coming down with a bad cold and a fever.

"Scott," I gasped, "what happened? Grandma was looking all over for you." My voice took on a menacing tone. "WHERE WERE YOU? Tell me."

"Why, I was just waiting for you, Grandma. What took you so long? You look as though you've been swimming in a river. Don't look so worried. I won't tell my mommy that you were late."

Grandma Iris

Sometimes It's Great to Be a Grandmother!

Being a grandmother has numerous benefits. It solves the dilemma of a son-in-law or daughter-in-law with a mental block about calling us "Mom" or "Mother." They finally know how to address us. Instead of "Hello there," "Hi," or "My dear," we are now "Grandma."

We can brag about the family and the children and get away with it (if we don't overdo it).

We have our special place at the table and everybody knows it.

We can see the children during the day and sleep through the night.

We can be a guest instead of a hostess.

When things go wrong, we often are asked to help, and we soon discover grandmothers have a way of making order out of chaos.

We can get plenty of fresh air and exercise in all seasons while we navigate a baby carriage, run after a child, push a swing or balance a seesaw in the playground.

We find that our grandchildren are easy to relate to. They don't argue, talk back or keep us waiting.

We are insulated against occasional bouts of loneliness. We can pick up the phone and call a daughter or daughter-in-law about visiting the grandchildren.

We stay younger in body and spirit by entering our grandchildren's world. We take them for long walks and help them learn to ride their bicycles. We read books to our grandchildren, listen to their records, cheer for their team or hero, and watch TV cuddled on the sofa with them.

We don't have to try so hard anymore. We have no more mountains to climb, no miles to go before we sleep. We can enjoy spectator sports, take a long-dreamed-of vacation, spend time with our friends, dawdle over lunch, have telephone visits and get up-to-date on what's happening in other people's lives—even if it's gossip!

Children who don't have a grandmother may look longingly at those who do. My 9-year-old grandson was playing with a friend. The child searched my face with big, sad eyes. He touched my arm and asked me softly, "Will you be my grandmother, too? I don't have any."

I hugged him and said, "Well, you've got one now. You can start calling me 'Grandma.'" An award for bravery, beauty and brilliance would not have meant as much to me as my grandson's reaction that moment. He smiled gratefully and said, "I don't know what kind of a mother you were, but you are a TERRIFIC grandmother." Sometimes it's great to be a grandmother!

Margaret B.

3
Who Said Grandmothers Prefer Tea to Gin?

Myths About Grandmothers

Since ancient times, the image of the ideal grandma has been that of an elderly woman with an ample bosom, spectacles, a kindly face, pleasant wrinkles, and graying or white hair held in a bun by silvery hairpins. Her uniform has comprised sensible shoes, non-sheer stockings, a firm corset and a proper brassiere. Her standard possessions have included a cameo brooch, a string of pearls, crystal beads and a gold timepiece on a long chain.

Ideally, Grandma lives in a picture-book house with a porch and a garden. The house is in the country and is set back from the road. Inside, time stands still. Sunlight filters through the lace curtains. The piano is draped with a silk-fringed shawl. Photographs of family members at different ages rest on the tables. There is an ever-present aroma of vanilla and cinnamon.

It is also acceptable for grandmothers to live in large, comfortable apartments. These apartments expand like magic to accommodate any number of family members, who of course are always welcome. The furnishings and pictures in the apartment are just like those in the house in the country. Nothing ever needs to be refurbished. Everything always remains the same. The charm of grandmotherhood is this simplicity and sense of serenity.

Ideally, grandmothers are never too busy to stop whatever they are doing to spend time with their children and grandchildren. They don't have other plans or *that* many things to occupy them. Ask any grandmother, she'll tell you. They have endless time, tea and sympathy, and pocket money.

Grandmothers are seldom career women. Rarely are they working on projects that could make them rich and famous. (Some exceptions are allowed, of course.) They seldom have independent viewpoints, and get their ideas from their husbands or the media. A grandmother is never very smart, athletic, assertive, romantic or eccentric.

Here are some other myths about grandmothers:

Grandmothers love to keep busy. When they come to visit, it's a good idea to have "pick-up" work handy (mending, ironing).

Grandmothers love family picnics and scenic drives in the country. A grandmother fits comfortably in the back seat with the picnic basket, the soft drinks, the dog and the children. She loves having the little ones draped over her while she opens a drink for the thirsty one, peels an apple for the one who gets carsick and holds a plastic container for the one who has to make wee-wee. Grandmothers are delighted when the grandchildren fight over who will sit next to her. She appreciates the pastoral scenery and hopes the day will never end.

Grandmothers enjoy going to the zoo. They don't mind swollen feet on a hot summer day while they limp from one refreshment stand to another getting ice cream and frankfurters for the children. Having a few "sit-downs" with "feet-ups" is the greatest fun. Not taking one's eyes off the grandchildren for a second is a joy.

Grandmothers have been waiting all their lives to have full responsibility for their grandchildren. They aren't the least bit intimidated by the prospect of feeding, bathing and diapering the newborn baby.

Grandmothers don't mind being alone. They are not afraid of lightning, thunder, hurricanes, blizzards or things that go bump in the night. They can weather any storm and always make the right decision.

Grandmothers have no personal secrets and need no privacy. Locking the door or knocking on it is not necessary. What could an older person possibly want to keep to herself?

Grandmothers love to be asked to cook. Nothing gives them greater pleasure than baking cakes and preparing platters for parties their families give. Of course, they aren't interested in socializing with the guests.

Grandmothers are gentle tyrants. They are warm, lovable and easygoing, yet full of forewarnings and forebodings. They are simple little old ladies who can make 6-foot sons and powerful executives tremble.

Grandmothers never throw anything away. They save all kinds of little things that surely will come in handy one fine day.

Grandmothers prefer living like hermits. They don't enjoy the clatter of family life. Just give them peace, quiet and solitude. They appreciate long stretches of isolation, uninterrupted even by telephone calls. They appreciate time for thinking!

Grandmothers love decaffeinated coffee. They never drink any stimulant, and wouldn't dream of touching alcohol.

Grandmothers don't like exercise. Only young grandmothers enjoy pushing a baby carriage through the park or riding a bicycle with the baby strapped in a carrier.

Grandmothers are not fashion-conscious. They wear sensible shoes so they can stand comfortably while baking in the kitchen. They prefer support hose to panty hose by Hanes. And no grandmother would think of going without a bra!

Grandmothers do not read or understand the stock market and bond reports in the newspaper. They avoid independent investments in real estate. They are not interested in knowing the interest rates on their savings accounts. They find it impossible to balance their checkbooks.

Grandmothers enjoy going to supermarkets. They get the best free samples there.

Grandmothers find aging a pleasant experience. They just drift into it and don't think much about it.

Grandmothers never use profanity. Vulgar language has no place in their vocabulary (except for biblical phrases). No four-letter words ever pass their lips. (They don't even understand what those words mean!)

Grandmothers have only the purest thoughts. When they look contemplative or wear a Mona Lisa smile, it is not because they are entertaining carnal fantasies or remembering an old romance.

Grandmothers are never forgetful. When they put something away for safekeeping, they carefully write a little note to themselves and also tell someone they trust about where they put this treasure.

Grandmothers' feelings aren't easily hurt. Grandmothers are such understanding people that they can accept and deal with any slight or oversight.

Grandmothers are always content. They maintain an ever-smiling countenance. They never feel angry, irritated, dissatisfied or unhappy.

FREE

Favorite Grandchildren?

We're not supposed to have a favorite.
But there's always one whose smile tugs at our heart.
There's always one who hugs us whenever we come.
There's always one who is the very image of our son or daughter as
    a child.
And what about the fighter?
And the angry one?
And the croupy one who stops crying when we hold him or her?
What about the demanding one, the attention-getter or the tease?
And the slob.
There's the one who wants to hear all about the family history.
And will look at old photo albums with us.
And see the resemblances.
There's the one who knows to phone when we are alone.
The one who is away and then comes home.

We love them all. We watch them grow and develop into the
people we hoped they would become. We keep in touch on
birthdays, graduations and holidays. We call just to say "Hello,"
just to let them know we are part of their lives, and that they will
stay part of ours.

It is unfair to ask children whom they love best, Mommy or
Daddy. It is just as unfair to ask Grandma which grandchild she
loves best. She is supposed to resist having favorites. Chances are
she will sidestep the question. "They are all the same to me, but
when Roger hugs me, it's a wonder my bones don't crack. He
knows how to hug a grandma. When Debbie smiles, it's
summertime. Mitchell always says, 'Let's not start to eat until
Grandma sits down with us.'" Nevertheless, many grandmothers
have favorites at different times for different reasons.

It's a Pleasure

My daughter invited me to her women's consciousness-raising group. I knew they regarded me as a relic of bygone days who had some unusual modern ideas. The group, out of politeness, asked me to honor them by opening the discussion with a few words on my attitudes toward sex. I stood up, made sure all eyes were on me, glanced at my daughter and said clearly, "It's a pleasure!"

Once upon a time I would have been uncomfortable talking about sex. I knew that what I might say wasn't necessarily autobiographical, but would others? People just don't think of grandmothers as sexual. Yet, how did we ever get pregnant and have two, three, five or eight children? When we talked in whispers among ourselves, was it only to exchange recipes? I remember we often talked about myth-breaking subjects, including where, when and how to get abortions. Our mutual concerns weren't so different from those of women today.

Once upon a time if a woman enjoyed sex and admitted it, or, even worse, said it was not just something to be "tolerated," she was not genteel. She was just plain "no good." Today there is no shortage of grandmothers like myself who believe that sex is the greatest thing since lipstick and sliced bread—and we are here to stay.

Marian C.

Must Grandmothers . . . ?

Look like Whistler's mother, not Marlene D.?
Have well-upholstered bosoms, never go bra-free?
Seem suited to aprons rather than jeans?
Use Ivory soap and leave "Charlie" to teens?

Tote family photos, not "Playgirl" or "Penthouse?"
Adore little babies, not another dame's spouse?
Sit in a rocker and sing lullabies?
Knit tiny booties and look very wise?

Enjoy Yardley's soap, long for red roses,
Monogrammed hankies, wipe drippy noses?
Want heavy charm bracelets, warm robes and white blouses
And other such gifts to clutter their houses?

Elaine B.

4
The
Other Grandmother

We don't choose all our relatives; our children choose some of them for us. They fall in love, but there is no guarantee their mums will have the same feelings toward one another. That first encounter may be surprisingly pleasant ("as if we've always known each other ") or it may be disappointing ("not my type at all. No way").

Each mum extends her antennae, dons her armor and puts her best ancestral foot forward. Both women try to be the embodiment of felicity and good will, with a touch of reserve. The couple in love watches anxiously for encouraging signs. But usually it takes time for the relationship between mothers to develop, for better or worse. Meanwhile, everyone hopes for the best.

Little attention has been paid to the subject of the other grandmother, or the combination of other grandmothers that children might have in this modern age. When grandmothers get along, it promotes family harmony. It's a good omen. It isn't possible to understand another person completely. But it is prudent and practical to try to understand the other grandmother(s).

One question for the future is: What will it be like between the mums when the grandchildren arrive? No matter how different, most mothers get along quite well as grandmothers. They may never be friends, just friendly relatives—sort of. Frequently, they have the highest regard for one another. In any case, both are destined to share grandmotherly concerns and moments of great joy.

Each grandmother will smile when a little grandchild, with an entrancing display of affection, climbs up and sits on her lap without being told or forced to do it.

But there may be problems, too. Many grandmothers feel heartbroken if the *other grandmother* seems to be the favorite. It's important to remember that the grandchild's feelings may be more than a matter of chemistry. Sometimes the child sees one grandmother more often because that grandmother lives closer. It's hard for a child to love someone from a distance.

Nevertheless, the popularity of the other grandmother can lead to agonizing self-doubt.

Just because the other grandmother knits sweaters and booties without looking and I'm all thumbs, am I inferior? All she's doing is moving her fingers. Right?

Just because I am in the bathroom mopping the floor after the baby vomited and the other grandmother breezes in with hat and gloves, reeking of Arpege, am I a peasant and is she a queen?

Just because the other grandmother is a career woman with an answering service and I list my occupation as *housewife*, am I a nobody?

Just because the other grandmother is well-endowed and I'm slender, will the grandchildren prefer putting their heads on her large bosom rather than my smaller one?

The answer to these questions is *no*! My friend Gloria explained the situation very well.

"At *my house* there are genuine early American reproductions, sturdy nylon carpeting and informality," she said. "Our mutt, Sylvester, lounges on the floor near the rocking chair. The once-a-week cleaning lady is old and feeble, but a good friend.

"At *my house* it's only plastic table mats, stainless steel, solid stemless glasses. The aroma is likely to be meat loaf, baked potatoes, pale string beans, wilted lettuce. The glossy store-bought fruit pie and petits fours in ruffled paper cups attest to my unmistakable deficits," Gloria continued, grinning. "My luggage is dark-green, wipe-clean vinyl, and my shoes are more sturdy than stylish. To me, the grandchildren are special little people who need freedom and space.

"At *her house* it's a different story. The linen absolutely glistens and the crystal sparkles. Sterling flatware, a floral centerpiece, mints and salted nuts grace the table. The aroma of roasting turkey, honeyed yams and a golden apple pie (the product of a wizard) give pause for admiration and envy. There are no limits to the other grandmother's perseverance."

Gloria shook her head in wonder. "The furniture, original paintings and ivory figurines are, of course, out of bounds for the children. To her, grandchildren are much-loved trained pets, and if you ask me, that's exactly the way they behave when they are with her. They stand poised on the border of the lounge like her two terriers, never putting a foot in the forbidden territory.

"Yet, to be fair, everything declares good taste, graciousness and quiet efficiency. Oh! Did I mention that her luggage is saddle-stitched leather? Her handbags from Gucci? I can't compete. Compared to the other grandmother, I am just a sparrow in God's universe."

70

Despite these differences, Gloria and the other grandmother get along very well.

"With the special wisdom of grandmothers, we find a quiet corner to talk," Gloria said. "The other grandmother and I know which grandchild is the prodigy, which one already has problems, the one whose health is frail, the one who will always succeed, and the 'spoiled' one. Sometimes we exchange a few philosophical sighs, vexations and satisfactions, but never recipes.

"So what if she has a penchant for elegance?"

As Gloria points out, being a grandmother is not competitive. No matter how different they are, both grannies have the best interests of their grandchildren at heart. Because they will probably meet at birthday parties and other family affairs, they will have opportunities to transcend their differences and really become acquainted. They may even like one another and find they have no basic disagreements.

However, despite everyone's best efforts, things may not always go smoothly. The following voices describe how women's love for their grandchildren sometimes has helped overcome these difficulties.

> *The other grandmother and myself have tried and tried to develop a relationship or even keep up a conversation. Now we expect nothing more than low-level conversation, such as, "How are things?" or "What's new?" All we seem to have in common are her daughter's marriage to my son, our mutual experience of hysterectomies and airsickness. Even our blood pressures are extremes. Hers is high, mine is low. Yet, between us there's a baby we both love who brings us together without so much as lifting a little finger.*
>
> *Millie P.*

I don't want to sound unkind or critical, but the other grandmother is stingy. What a penny pincher. She wouldn't give ice away in the winter. Her generosity is limited to lip service, a "God bless you" when you sneeze. She knows about great bargains, but can't remember the name of the store. Her recipes sound elegant and expensive—at least 10 eggs, pure butter, sweet cream and so on. I'm sure she uses substitutes. An ingredient is always missing.

When someone asks for a charity contribution, she does some hard breathing and has a sudden hearing problem. Oh, and does that woman know how to count! When she goes on vacation, unless there's a committee of at least six to see her off, she's disappointed. As a grandmother she's all talk, no motion. However, despite all this, the family caters to this woman. I can't figure out why. Maybe I should try her tactics just to see how it feels. But what's the use? I wish I could, but I can't. Which is probably one of the reasons I talk to myself quite a lot.

Jean L.

I've told my children, "Don't expect me to be on call at the drop of a hat like the other grandmother. I'll do many things for you, but no child-minding at home. I'll take the kids on trips, have them for visits (not all at once, please), even go with them to the circus—the ultimate in grandmotherly endurance, considering the noise, crowds, smells, transportation, steps, going to the toilet and retrieving sweaters that have fallen down several levels."

Doris L.

The other grandmother's world revolves around the grandchildren. They are her greatest joy. For her, nothing can match being with the babies. "Call me any time," she tells the children, "day or night, I'll get there . . ."

I love my grandchildren, too, but there are also other things in the world I enjoy. Unlike Rose, grandchildren don't constitute the 'all' of my life. I enjoy the happiness my children get from their children and their life together. They know I'll answer the call if I'm needed.

Amy T.

The other grandmother? The truth? Her name is Grizelda. It's ugly, and suits her perfectly. Our relationship is a total washout. Our dislike for one another was instantaneous and instinctive. Between us there is arctic silence. For the sake of the children, we have stopped grinding our teeth at family gatherings. Get the picture? I don't understand how such an unlovely person can have such a lovely daughter.

Roslyn M.

The other grandmother, Marcia, has the mistaken idea that everyone else is as interested in her grandchildren as she is. She puts the baby close to the telephone and says, "Stevie, darling, say 'Hello' to Grandma's friend, Auntie Bertha. Bertha, say 'Hello' to Stevie . . ."

Bertha B.

Geraldine and I were best friends. The only time we competed was in a spelling bee. (Only someone over 45 will remember what that was.) We never dreamed that one day we would be grandmothers parading our mutual grandchildren in baby carriages. But ours was destined to be a prolonged union. Her daughter married my son and our grandchildren have a built-in guarantee that they will have loving grandmothers. I brag endlessly about the other grandmother's artistic talent and awards. She only brags about our gorgeous grandsons, born 15 months apart.

One afternoon we were sitting on a park bench, just two nice grannies chatting away, eyes focused on their little grandsons playing on the grass. A woman walking by paused to listen to their delicious gurgle of laughter. She smiled indulgently at our bovine expressions. "They are adorable," she said. "Are they your grandchildren?" I nodded, but Geraldine said loudly, "Oh yes! Thank you. They belong to us. Aren't they beautiful? They are angelic and so clever. Brilliant, really. You wouldn't believe the things they say and do." Awed by this outburst, the woman smiled and said, "Of course. Anyone can see that at a glance. They could almost be twins, but apparently they aren't. How old are they?" Before I could answer, the other grandmother said proudly, "The doctor is the 4-year-old. The computer scientist is only 3."

Melanie S.

The other grandmother is to be admired. SHE can say in two minutes what it takes me 20 to say. SHE can write a comprehensive family news report in one paragraph. With me it becomes a book. Everything SHE does is precise and economical. SHE can get her wishes across clearly. I founder while trying to be diplomatic. Every cake of HERS is foolproof. SHE follows recipes the way chemists follow formulas. By comparison, most of what I do tends to be excessive.

HER reactions are controlled, reasonable. Mine are volatile and spontaneous. SHE has physical endurance. I fade. Why compete? There are really no battles for us to fight and no prizes to be won.

Doris R.

Since she became a grandmother, Vera's days begin and end with the grandchildren. Unlike me, she even sleeps at night with a symbol of her grandmotherhood. The clank of her grandmother bracelet and the little gold locket with locks of her grandchildren's curls in it are never far from her person. The photographs are on the night table beside her. Just the same, as grandmothers, we can laugh comfortably together about our differences. Between us there is no rivalry. Between us we inherit the world.

Sophia L.

Beyond a shadow of a doubt, the other grandmother and I are cut from different cloth. You can eat off her floor. I wouldn't recommend eating off mine. She enjoys TV soap operas and talk shows. I prefer documentaries and ballet. She drinks weak lemon tea. I'm crazy about strong black coffee, and don't mind it with a dash of Irish whiskey. Although our interests are not totally compatible, our mutual concern for family and tradition is reverent and steadfast.

Ruthie K.

The other grandmother is a problem. She constantly alludes to the marriage of her daughter to my son as a crime committed against herself and her daughter's expectations. This has led to grievances, innuendoes and inferences.

She makes it seem as if her daughter, Sandra, the beauty with brains from a lovely family of means, deserved someone better than my Arthur. Someone richer, who would see that diamonds and furs were hers for the asking. She is convinced that our son misled the girl into believing he was a man of wealth and importance. Now, after several years, a happy marriage and three children, the other grandmother still has a classic case of resentment. She never changes, still throwing out words like stones. But for the sake of the children, I ignore her remarks. Personally, I think my son is a saint to put up with her nonsense. What else can I tell you?

Bess L.

Comparisons can be unnerving. Being a grandmother is not a competitive enterprise or popularity contest. Pity the grandmother whose child is facing divorce. She sees that she may have to pitch in and help her son or daughter start over again. Who else can help out in a single-parent household, or, heaven forbid, in a household with no parents? Maybe that's why God made grandmothers.

If those who say nasty things about grandmothers are ever arraigned in a heavenly court, grandmothers will not appear at the trial. They will be too busy picking up their grandchildren after school, taking them to the doctor or a music lesson, or baby-sitting at home.

Not all grandmothers answer the call with a good heart or generous spirit. But it is astonishing how far a grandmother will go and how much she will do for the sake of her children and grandchildren. This even extends to trying to develop a relationship with the other grandmother, even though she may have little in common with her at first.

Over the years, differences between the grandmothers become less important. Each has found reasons to believe the other grandmother's heart is in the right place. They have trod much the same path. As the grandchildren become older, the grandmothers have the same mixed feelings—sadness and relief. They no longer have to feel guilty that perhaps they aren't doing enough. They enjoy times when there is nothing they *have* to do. For both grandmothers, commitment and loyalty to family remain steadfast. As one grandmother said to another, "Believe me, there's nothing like blood, Helen. And don't you forget it!"

The Absentee Grandmother

I'm an absentee grandmother. This means I live a great distance from my children and grandchildren. A visit is no small exercise in time management and logistics.

It was my first grandchild's first birthday. Would I miss it? Not on your life! I traveled halfway across the world and ached with happiness as I held that youngster and kissed him over and over again. Then came the day of the party.

I couldn't wait to get to my daughter's apartment. It was clear at once that almost everyone there belonged to my son-in-law's family. The house was vibrating with festivity and joy. The other grandmother was taking photographs, and each one would be absolutely wonderful. Everything she did was always done well. I watched the other grandmother, this competent woman who lived only 20 minutes away from our mutual grandson.

Everyone fussed about me for a little while and then went about the business of being at a family gathering. I made some brief forays into the conversations, but an increasing sense of isolation and some kind of grief was taking hold of me. What were my triennial visits compared to her weekly or daily visits made with loving dedication? "I don't deserve any more than I am getting," I said to myself miserably. I became totally immersed in self-pity, invisibility, as the other grandmother took over. I was now a dot on the horizon, becoming smaller and smaller.

Little Daniel was dressed in a knitted wool suit (she knitted it). I had sent a check. On the table was a flowered cloth the O.G. (Other Grandmother) had embroidered with, "Happy Birthday, Daniel," plus a cute clown offering lollipops and striped peppermint sticks. Golden hands? Unbelievable! She was an artist to her fingertips. She had arranged for an astonishingly large birthday cake decorated with proper credentials and creamy flowers. What was left for me—the "absentee grandmother"—to do but collect dirty dishes or pour drinks? I stood there with all the others singing, "Happy Birthday," clapped when Mommy and Daddy blew out the candles, and then wended my way to the kitchen. Where else does a useless appendage at a party go?

Platters of sandwiches and salads decorated with florets of parsley arranged by the O.G. confronted me. My daughter was trying to loosen the jello mold while I folded paper napkins. "Deliver me," I prayed silently. Suddenly, I heard my daughter call, "Mom, come here quickly, Mom, I need you. Help!"

My heart leaped. She needs me! At last I have a purpose. "What is it, darling?" I asked as I ran to where she was, huddled over the kitchen sink. I was literally breathless with gratitude. "Not you," she shrieked, "I mean my other mother!"

My first impulse was to take the jello mold that only the O.G. could unmold and throw it away. My next impulse was to run, but only after lashing out at my daughter and the O.G. who had usurped my prerogatives, my grandmotherly rights and legitimate claims to usefulness! By God, that O.G. was my enemy!

Tears welled up. I could hear those famous last words, "I mean my other mother." Since when did my daughter have another mother? I was nothing more than a piece of driftwood washed up on some lonely kitchen-floor tiles.

I managed to slink away towards the bathroom. I quietly closed the door and locked it. I cried, berated myself, carried on an inaudible dialogue with my daughter and the O.G., let my injured self-esteem assert itself, then tried to think of things to be happy about. I wiped my eyes on the monogrammed finger towels (also made by the O.G.). I looked in the mirror. "You are still the only mother—the only natural mother—my daughter has." I washed my face, put on some makeup and decided two things. First, I had raised a daughter who could appreciate a fine mother-in-law. Second, a grandmother can make the best and the most of every situation.

Enid A.

5
The Art of Baby-Sitting

What Is a Baby-Sitter?

A teen-ager with references who charges the going rate. Experienced in watching TV, raiding the refrigerator, playing games with children and talking on the telephone. Equipped with transistor radio.

Or

A middle-aged or elderly lady. Parents think of them as surrogate grandmothers, and sometimes they love like proper grandmothers, but they don't get nervous the way real grandmothers do. For them, sitting means pocket money, although sometimes it is also a much-loved hobby. Elderly sitters have rules. No dishes, no cooking, no mending, no folding laundry. They usually require a simple meal, with coffee or tea.

Or

Is there a grandmother in the house?

Some grandmothers are programmed for baby-sitting. These grandmothers include:

The one who comes for the weekend and finds that the parents want to give her as much time as possible with the grandchildren. They tell her this will enable her to get to know the grandchildren really well and to develop a "meaningful relationship" with the little ones.

The one who is there because she has nowhere else to go. She is a permanent fixture, because she has no choice. She is always available, whether she wants to be or not.

The one who can't think of a plausible excuse when her children phone.

The one who lives nearby and doesn't mind baby-sitting. She often finds that the children leave the silver polish and silver service in a conspicuous place, so she'll have something to do if she has spare time or starts to get bored.

The one who can't wait to be asked. She's been waiting for this all her married life. The mere thought fills her with anticipation and happiness. Baby-sitting times are her golden hours.

The one who doesn't hesitate if she can manage it. Her children are a priority in her life. She enjoys being a grandmother and knows she plays an important role in the lives of her grandchildren. She handles babies with ease. She also knows when to say "no." She tactfully gets the message across that the parents ought to stay home—or get someone else to baby-sit.

The one who is so glad she was asked. She can tell her friends how the grandchildren keep her busy. She would never tell anyone, but she finds that baby-sitting is a relief from premature retirement or drifting uselessly into old age. She surprises even herself with how resourceful she can be when coping with unexpected situations that arise while she is baby-sitting.

The one who baby-sits when she can. She will also baby-sit when she knows she is really needed, even though she would rather do something else. She's efficient, clearheaded, tender and affectionate. She's an angel of mercy who doesn't expect a reward. The little ones respond to her as naturally as to their mother—until the mother returns, anyway.

Help, Mom, Please!

Dear Mom,

I know you planned your vacation in Europe with Daddy, but I have to ask you to do something for me. Plainly, Mom, my marriage is on the rocks. The only way I can salvage it is to be with my husband alone, so he'll open up and I'll be able to talk to him. With the three children around, it's impossible. There's always something. Either it's too late, the children will hear, or he's too tired. I need help, Mom. Mom darling, I reserved a honeymoon cottage at a hotel in the mountains for a week. But Mom, it will be impossible unless you stay with the kids. Won't you please, PLEASE postpone your trip? I'm desperate.

> *Your suicidal daughter,*
> *Ruthie*

P.S. You are the only baby-sitter I can really trust. I love you!!

> *R.*

The Bitter Truths

When I'm baby-sitting, I bring to the task reliability and dedication no money can buy. I may be clumsy or handy, shaky on my feet or full of pep, suffering with migraine, but I'm still top-quality. No one has to feed me or get me home by 11 p.m. for tomorrow's exam. I arrive early, ready to start. Lucky me if the sink isn't full of dishes.

> *Naomi B.*

I get emotionally involved in whatever I do. That's my nature. I even take it personally when the baby vomits or the older one stares at me as if I'm a stranger and says, "I don't want YOU. I want my MOMMY."

Wilma G.

When I'm baby-sitting, I feel absolutely selfless and absorbed. A tornado can rip through the country a few miles away, but I'm worrying about whether the baby's bottle is too hot or too cold.

Fanny G.

It took a long time to learn not to bury myself in the kitchen. Believe me, food isn't everything. We can't make grandchildren fatter or healthier overnight. I don't ask what they want to eat. I'd go crazy. I give them what's there and sit down with them. If they don't eat, I tell myself, "Never mind, we'll all survive . . ."

Annie W.

A grandmother doesn't just SIT. When the little ones are fast asleep, I tiptoe in every few minutes to look, or collapse on the sofa nervously waiting for the sound of their parents. I'm even worried about going to the bathroom in case the baby calls, so I leave the bathroom door open.

Berdie C.

Baby-sitting is not what I imagined! I'm not allowed to help with the family wash, fix a meal or put the little ones to bed. When the family takes a vacation, a housekeeper-nanny is in charge of the children. My presence is purely political. Watch and say nothing, lest the sainted mother feel her job is being usurped. If she walks out, I'm in big trouble.

The last time I was asked to "just be around in case" and "not to interfere," I overheard the housekeeper-nanny tell her friend on the telephone that "in the future, I don't want any grandmothers interfering." That's fine, I thought to myself. In the future, when my children ask me to baby-sit, I'll tell them, "Certainly, on the condition that the housekeeper-nanny is not there to boss me around, as if I were one of the kids." The result? They still prefer the housekeeper-nanny. After all, she's there when I'm not. If she isn't there, they know they can always bring the children to me. Either way, I'm odd-woman-out.

Rose G.

It was a good summer. Never got to the Japanese cooking class. Never took the hike. The best part was the family, and constant reassurance that they liked having me close by. We took short trips together. One weekend they took my apartment and I took their house. Had a great time with the four children, but my son noted that I broke all baby-sitter records for fast takeoffs when they returned.

Genevieve G.

I don't want to be a "battered grandmother." When my grandchildren are fighting and throwing things, I keep a safe distance. They're not likely to get hurt, but I might. They do this all the time. I can't solve the problem of sibling rivalry. Threats make me the enemy. Concern for my headache may stop the action. If not, I stay calm and wait it out. If the situation gets out of control, I promise them ANYTHING their parents can afford.

I retreat from the field and let them come to terms. They can be really rough with each other. But try to say one word against one to the other, and they attack me, or worse, ignore me. I learned not to underestimate the depth of their relationship when they close ranks.

Judith F.

From my experience—and I've had plenty, with five grandchildren—there is no harm in being prepared. So I carry baby aspirin, cough-drop lollipops and a rectal thermometer. The doctor always asks, "How much temperature?" Whether I'm sitting an hour, a day, a week or a month, a child ALWAYS gets something—a sore throat, a rash, an upset stomach—or falls on his head. I can never find what I need in someone else's medicine cabinet.

Julie W.

My grandchildren are the best in the world, God bless them, but I never trust them to be on MY side. The baby can't report on what I do or don't do, but the older ones tell on me every time I give them more ice cream than allowed or let them stay up late to watch TV. When my daughter says, "Mother! Shame on you!" I feel like a disgraced grandmother.

Evelyn A.

I learned the hard way. I entered the "world of the child," just as the book says. I thought they expected me to be an athlete. We played hide-and-seek. I got under the coffee table, needed help to get up and physiotherapy to get back on my feet.

Sarita J.

I answer the call when I'm needed. I stick to the job and don't look for trouble. I don't inspect, snoop, rearrange things or look for dust under the bed. I come and go.

Shoshana H.

I don't claim to have done the best job with my own children and I don't mind learning new ways. It's a good idea to give children some relief from parents or teachers. Maybe I spoil my grandchildren, but I like being someone they confide in and trust. I don't try to improve their characters. I work on my own, and that's enough of a project.

Frances L.

Puzzlements

Q. I get along better with my grandchildren than I did with my own children. Why?

A. You don't have to live with them. (Even if you do, you're still not the boss.)

Q. My grandchildren get along better with me than with their parents. Why?

A. See previous answer.

Q. My grandchildren confide to me things they hesitate to tell their parents. Why?

A. Because parents are for soap, shoulds and should-nots. Grandmothers are for solace, secrets and sweets.

Q. I'm more open-minded with my granddaughter Nan than I was with my own daughter. Why?

A. You weren't separated from Nan's umbilical cord.

Q. I use a package of diapers a day. My daughter uses a package a week. Why?

A. What your daughter doesn't know is that a grandmother can see a rash before it breaks out.

Q. A grandmother witnesses and knows so much, but how can you pass it on without being told, "MO...THER, you're interfering," or even worse, getting an icy look, the thin-lipped treatment or silence?

A. The less you say, the less you'll have to take back. Humble pie is hard to swallow.

Q. After all that my daughters learned about the advantages of breast-feeding a baby, both decided not to go ahead with it. Why?

A. The reason is simple. They can leave the baby and the bottle with Grandma.

Q. My grandchildren have tantrums at home, but never in Grandma's house? Why?

A. Because they don't have to test Grandma the way they constantly test their parents. Grandma is there for two reasons: to love and to feed.

Q. Why do I feel I could manage the grandchildren and the house better than my daughter does?

A. Because you live 1,500 miles away.

Q. When my little granddaughter got a splinter in her foot, it wasn't easy to accept the fact that she believed only Mommy or Daddy could remove it, not Grandma. Why?

A. Wait. There will be other opportunities for your granddaughter to learn that sometimes Grandma knows best—or at least as much as Mommy and Daddy.

Q. When my little grandson ceases to get undressed in front of me for his bath, does that mean the beginning of the end of our relationship?

A. Ease up, Grandma! The child is diplomatically indicating he has reached another stage in his development. At least you're still in the bathroom!

Q. Our children insist we spend the weekend at their place and "enjoy" the grandchildren. Their "place" is a two-bedroom apartment with one bathroom. The apartment is on the 15th floor. We just happen to be phobic about elevators. They also have two cats that we're allergic to. What should we do?

A. Don't go. You need that like a moose needs a hatrack.

Joys of Baby-Sitting

You're fresh from the hairdresser, all aglow and feeling great. You think you look terrific, and the little one asks, "Hey, Grandma, how come you've got a mustache?"

Disconcerting comments aside, being involved with a baby does wonderful things for our appearance. It makes us feel special, easing our aches and pains and smoothing our wrinkles.

In time, we apparently begin to look like proper grandmothers. People address us as "Mother" or "Granny." Older mothers tell us they wish their children still had a grandmother or they wish they had known their own grandmothers better. We are forgiven if we doze during a conversation or a performance just as long as we don't snore.

All this indicates that it's OK to ask a stranger to carry our shopping basket to the car or give up a seat on the bus.

Guidelines for Grandmothers

Loving our grandchildren is natural and enjoying our grand-children is a blessing. But all grandmothers should remember these two basic rules:

Don't haggle or bargain for affection. Asking for kisses is asking for trouble. If the grandchildren refuse, we might become involved in a battle. There are stages and ages. Kissing the baby is delicious and uncomplicated. Hugs are special. But when we feel our grandchildren squirming, we shouldn't feel heartbroken. They're just growing up.

Don't pinch!

106

6
The Visit

We're Coming to Visit, All of Us!
Don't Panic!
Where There Is Room in the Heart,
There Is Room in the House!

My first grandchild's visit was only the beginning. For that first little person, barely 3 weeks old, our house was transformed by additional furniture and equipment. We borrowed a crib, bought a folding carriage and baby supplies. A changing table was outfitted with paraphernalia that put an operating theater to shame. Grandpa turned up the thermostat for extra warmth. Forget about Grandma's menopausal hot flashes, anything for the sake of the baby. In time, as more grandchildren appeared on the scene, a visit found us prepared with playpen, swing, plastic swimming pool and rocking horse. Little clothes appeared in the closet; my desk was moved from the extra room to make way for the extra cot, doll carriage, and electric trains with their tracks and switches. Wherever the electric trains were, Grandpa and my son-in-law were sure to be. And wherever my grandchildren are going to be, I want to be close enough to have them visit and hear them ask, "Grandma, how ya doin?"

Doreen P.

How other grandmothers take the joys of their grandchildren's visits is their business. For me, as a grandmother and former schoolteacher, preparing for them is something of a project. I clear my work schedule, lay things out, organize what I will need. I don't believe that grandmother who says she doesn't do "a thing" before or after a visit. Little grandchildren bear a strong resemblance to a miniature demolition squad, regardless of upbringing. It will be a busy day after they leave. Cleaning up will take the sharp edge off the quiet and the abrupt emptiness that sends me scurrying to the telephone asking about the ride home and telling them how much I already miss them.

Mildred K.

Grandchildren may get excited about coming to my house, but they don't expect me to be exciting. Even if I were famous (which I'm not), internationally recognized (I can fantasize), well-traveled (would I love that!) or had dined with Princess Grace in Monaco (she was so friendly), what my grandchildren really care about—and I know it—is how I come across to THEM, not the rest of the world.

Rita P.

I like to recall how wonderful it is to see the happy little faces, hear the screen door slam and then their voices calling from one end of the house to the other. It is equally wonderful to breathe the silence when they go home. Now the inventory begins. Only two plates broken this time. So it's no longer a service for 12. The ice-cream stains on the carpet can be treated. From now on, food only in the kitchen! It was an accident that the ball hit the fish tank and the cat was faster than I was. How did the baby find Grandpa's keys and throw them in the toilet? The neighbors I can handle with a bottle of wine. They'll forget that the Doberman the children took for a walk left a souvenir on their front lawn.

It is something else to shut out the picture of a toddler falling down a flight of stairs and the terror that fills the heart when the doctor says, "A possible concussion." It's not easy to bring the child home with one leg in a plaster cast. I tremble when the scar over my little granddaughter's eye reminds me of the near-tragedy that happened when she stayed with me for a visit.

Agnes P.

Goodies are fine, but what counts is strength, an easy manner and warmth. Why try too hard and wear myself out at the altars of kitchen sink and oven? Kids aren't impressed with my quiche Lorraine or fondue. It's the hamburgers and french fries with lots of ketchup, the applesauce, cookies and drinks that make me an instant "Supergrandmother."

Julie S.

I was asked how I had enjoyed the visit of my grandchildren. "What!?" I cried. "Enjoyed?! I never left the kitchen. Everything I made was a work of art and all wrong. I prepared potatoes with dill, leg of lamb, a broccoli soufflé, cranberry sherbet and petits fours. They wanted french fries, frankfurters and Coca Cola. Every breakfast had to be pancakes. I am EXHAUSTED, and this is only the third day. My darling little grandchildren are little dictators.

Hilda R.

Why am I, the experienced veteran grandmother, tearful instead of cheerful when I kiss the grandchildren goodbye? It's not true that nothing dries faster than a tear. After the visit I may feel inclined to say, "Never again!" But I don't mean it. I love to remember their presence and the pleasure I experience when they say, "Grandma, everything tastes so delicious in your house. And you're delicious, too." That's why my memories are so sunny, and why our grandchildren can wind us around their little fingers.

Amy M.

"My world revolves around the grandchildren's visits. Bring them any time, or I'll come fetch them," my friend Ethel said. We feel differently about such visits. Life hasn't been easy for her, with a husband who is quite deaf and suffering from an incurable illness. "Let's face it," she said. "Two divorced daughters and one homosexual son is nothing to brag about. My other son's marriage to your daughter and the resulting grandchildren light up my life."

Ethel needs constant reassurance. "I still count my blessings, but believe me, sometimes if it weren't for the grandchildren's visits, I'm not sure whether I would want to go on." But no matter how down Ethel may be, a visit from the granchildren acts like a wonder drug. When they cross her threshold, Ethel's face becomes wreathed in smiles.

Bernice R.

112

I'm not overly thrilled about the grandchildren's visits unless they come with their parents and don't stay too long. I'm a high-strung person. Left alone with them, I worry about all sorts of things happening to them and what I would do "if." I wish a grandmother could take a course on How to Enjoy the Visits of Grandchildren. I bought Dr. Spock's book. He is on target with diagnoses and remedies, but he also emphasizes the need to trust your judgment. I tell myself that all the children need is to be fed, kept warm in the winter, cool in the summer and given lots of love. But what if they catch the flu or break out in a rash? When the parents leave them with me overnight, I put a little square of camphor wrapped in cloth on a string under their pajamas just to ward off colds, like my mother did. Babies are really best off at home with their parents; I just can't come to grips with the responsibility. I'm a total wreck when the visit is over.

Beatrice T.

Coming to Grandma's house was all fun and great anticipation. It was never ho-hum. But then everyone got busier. Visiting was inconvenient and rather difficult to fit in except for important family celebrations.

It's nice to save Grandma the wear and tear of preparations, but one has a nostalgic yearning for those faith-restoring days when family togetherness transcended a lot of other things. Nothing can replace the marvelous hectic atmosphere of family laughter—the noise and familiar voices in Grandma's house.

Justine's children gave her a beautiful 50th birthday party. They planned it for months. They made beautiful slides of her life history, including her school days, graduations, honeymoon, motherhood and grandmotherhood. They even had appropriate background music on tape. They planned the decorations, buffet supper, wines. Most important, the little grandchildren were there, and the guests were those Justine would have chosen.

I was one of the them. As the evening unfolded, a terrible sense of sadness came over me. My children lived miles and miles away. They couldn't visit me without making a long journey. The logistics were insurmountable.

I held back the tears, trying to share Justine's blessings and her children's love. Such care and painstaking thought had gone into making their mother happy. Her face was a picture of contentment.

Suddenly, overcome with emotion and self-pity, tears spilled over and down my face, as if floodgates had been opened. I ran from the party into the car and sobbed. My husband took me home while I poured out my anguish about living so far away from our children and grandchildren. I had so many regrets. As always, he was sensible and reassuring.

The next morning, Justine phoned. "I saw you leaving and I understood why. Believe me, it happened to me once when I lived far away from my parents and family. I knew what was going on in your mind. I saw it on your face last night."

"You're so lucky!" I cried. "You have your son living 20 minutes away. You have your grandchildren almost every weekend. You go there, or they come to you. I haven't seen my grandchildren in eight months. They hardly know I exist. What kind of a weird grandmother am I? They can't pop in for cookies or bring their friends to Grandma's house. I don't take them to the beach or fix hamburgers for them. You, Justine, are a proper grandmother. I am a failure. I have no desire to scratch the face of eternity with some incredible accomplishment. All I want is to be a credible grandmother, one they will look forward to seeing, and will remember with affection."

"Bite your tongue!" Justine said. "Sure. I do have them every weekend. Yes, every single weekend. Joe and I haven't had a weekend to ourselves for months. The parents drop the children off with the dog as if there were nothing else we'd rather do. 'Enjoy them, love you!' they call, and drive off.

"We are exhausted. They are lovely children, but we need a break. We need to retreat for an uninterrupted weekend—no sweeping mud off the kitchen floor and no thirsty little throats to wet late in the night.

"The party was last night. The darlings piled in an hour ago. I'm standing here with my hands in water when I'd like to be sitting under a beach umbrella on a remote Pacific island with a book. I'd settle for something as soothing as grating cheese. You don't know how lucky you are.

"Just remember, dear friend, that the grass only SEEMS greener in the next person's yard. There's a gap between what you see and what really exists. So, Erica, dry your tears. Write to your kids. Elevate your status as a grandmother. Tell them you're on the way. Tell them to get a big welcome ready because you need it very much. And then GO! Of course, you may come back sooner than you expected."

Erica A.

7
Presents Perfect

What did you bring? Grandma and presents go together like love and marriage, a horse and carriage. We love giving presents, but they don't take the place of love. A present doesn't open the door to the heart.

"There was a time when I really thought I wouldn't go into the house without a present in my hand or in my pocketbook. I know better now," said Jenny, a veteran grandmother. "When they ask, 'What did you bring?' I give them a huge smile, shoulders straight back, chest out, and say, 'Just me, Grandma!' When I ring the doorbell, they come shrieking down the steps yelling, 'Grandma's here!' By golly, all they want is me, Grandma Jenny!"

When grandparents take a vacation, Grandma frequently doesn't enjoy herself until she has bought gifts for the grandchildren. "After many years and eight grandchildren, I still feel that way about it," said Edna. "My husband and I travel quite a lot. We used to lug gift packages from all over for the grandchildren. We wanted each to get a present in the right color. The one we bought the blue present for wanted red. The one we thought wanted green wanted yellow. Now we have the assembly-line approach. We found we could buy them all the same thing in the same color and tell them, 'Put your name on it, darling.' There is no substitute for common sense."

Only a grandmother would say it's worth making a trip to Switzerland because it's a good place to visit and buy things for children. All those adorable animals cards, elves, embroidered clothes, cuckoo clocks, and music boxes with lullabies, waltzes and yodeling. Only a grandmother would buy a music box. She doesn't have to wind it and listen to it!

"If you see what you like, tell Grandma," is a standard commercial ploy. Many salespersons use it. But it involves passing the buck. It means getting grandparents on the hook and parents off. It's sensible to stay away from stores that use this technique. It isn't easy for Grandma to pass up such reminders, but it is a way to avoid expensive commitments and to explode the shopkeepers' myth that children can always depend on Grandma's generosity, even if it sends her to the poorhouse. Who could afford to give all her grandchildren word processors or electronic games?

Once upon a time, not so many years ago, when grandmothers strolled through infants' and children's departments, they could buy wonderful pull toys, dolls and velvet-collared coats for little girls and boys. A bicycle had three speeds, a bell and a basket. Nowadays it has 10 speeds, to say nothing of all those extra gadgets. It is a stouthearted grandmother who can make the switch from buying delicate hand-stitched dresses to buying garments in bright-colored stretch fabrics.

Another problem grandmothers have is being realistic about their grandchildren. We tend to think they are bigger, more attractive and smarter than they really may be.

As one grandmother who works as a salesperson said: "I'm the best salesperson in the children's department of a large department store. I am also a grandmother, and I understand the woman who says, 'My little grandson is so big for his age' or 'My little granddaughter is petite, a little doll.' Most grandmothers buy size 6 when they should buy size 3. I try to steer them right.

"When it's toys, grandmothers cherish the notion that they are depriving the child by not buying a Fisher-Price activity toy. Infants are happier banging a wooden spoon on an enamel pot or ripping up old copies of the newspaper. A grandchild is, of course, 'unusual,' 'promising' or 'a genius.' That's why Grandma looks for gifts in the 8- to 10-year-olds' category when she should be in the 3- to 5-year-olds' category. Whatever happened to all those little geniuses when they grew up?"

This is not to say grandmothers never change. In a toy department of a specialty store catering to children up to 10 years of age, a grandmother was heard to ask where she could find educational toys for little girls. "Do you have something specific in mind?" the salesperson asked. "As a matter of fact, I do," said the lady. "I am interested in a doll with complete genitalia and body parts."

123

One situation grandmothers have to come to grips with is the reality of birthdays. Elaine told 8-year-old Alissa she had planned a special birthday celebration for her. "We'll go to the zoo and a fancy restaurant. You can choose your own present. We'll have the whole day together, just the three of us—Grandma, Grandpa and Alissa." The child looked astonished and shook her head sadly. "Grandma, what a silly idea!" she said. "Did you get it out of a book? We would be so bored without Mommy, Daddy and my brother. Just you, Grandpa and me? Forget it, Grandma, no way!"

What's the use of running if you're on the wrong road?

Grandmothers are most conscientious about a grandchild's birthday. It's always a cute card, a phone call, a present, the works.

It was Ronald's fifth birthday. Caroline had promised him a bicycle with training wheels. She spent hours at Ezra's Bicycle Shop choosing the best model in the right color. On Ronald's birthday the bicycle was delivered without the training wheels. The child took one look and ran out sobbing inconsolably. Frantically, Caroline called Ezra and demanded that he attach those training wheels immediately! It was Ezra's day off, but he did it anyway. Caroline watched little Ronald riding back and forth happily. She ran along next to him and breathlessly asked, "Sweetheart, who gave you that wonderful bicycle?" The child looked her straight in the eye and said, "Ezra!"

(Grandmothers are such wonderful people that their feelings aren't easily hurt.)

126

When we think back to another age, when buying presents or making them was a pleasure, we realize how much time we spend just *choosing* gifts. Wearily, we line up at the cashier's desk, then wait for the wrapping to be done. We note our increasing exhaustion and shrinking bank balance. All this erodes our patience. Lynn, one of these intrepid grandmothers, doesn't mince words. She said flatly, "After Christmas shopping for the six grandchildren last year, I felt like locking the front door and not leaving the house until the all-clear siren signaled that inflation was over."

Grandmothers buy two types of gifts: things the grandchildren need and things they don't. Despite this limited range, grandmothers spend an astonishing amount of time pondering and shopping for the perfect gifts. None of these mad dashes to the shopping mall the day before a grandchild's birthday! "I buy sensibly," said Kate. "When I see something just right for a grandchild, I buy it, wrap it, label it and put it away. I manage to be prepared for special occasions. No last-minute running from store to store during a heat wave, a rainy day, a blizzard or when my arthritis is acting up."

Young, well-to-do grandmothers usually spend money lavishly on themselves and their grandchildren. Older grandmothers rarely spend it on themselves. Many of us with limited funds will deprive ourselves to give a child something special.

Rich or poor, young or old, what we buy depends not only on financial circumstances but on our philosophy and our expectations about how members of families should relate to one another.

Bewildered or enthusiastic grandmothers may innocently choose a present that parents are supposed to assemble and then share with the child. "When I saw my son-in-law playing with the electric trains I bought for Johnny, and my grandson watching Daddy having all the fun, I knew I had made a mistake," Paula said. "When the battery in the expensive toy car wore out after an hour and the child wept and threw it in the garbage, that was another mistake. It taught me a lesson."

Some grandmothers learn fast. "I never look for bargain toys," Valerie said. "They rust, break easily and cut. My daughter would stop talking to me if that happened. Even if my grandchildren get excited about a cheap toy in the window, I don't give in. I had to learn to control my impulses."

"My policy is simple," said Joan. "The 2-year-old gets a truck big enough to sit on. His 10-year-old brother collects miniature cars. For him, the smaller the better. I don't give my 4-year-old granddaughter a little doll to dress. She's happier with one as big as herself that she can hug, cuddle and mother. What it amounts to is, the smaller the child, the bigger the toy."

Giving presents shouldn't be complicated. One solution is to give money or a check to the parents and tell them to buy something for the grandchildren from Grandma. Money itself doesn't delight young grandchildren. Money is paper to them. It's better to put the money in a bank account for them. The day will arrive when they will love it and thank you.

Grandmothers should also think about presents they can leave behind. Some people think the fact that we only own things temporarily is a gloomy thought. But for others, the idea of passing possessions along provides a sense of authority, identity and pride. "It's a good idea not to lose faith in property," said Beatrice, a great-grandmother who is approaching 70. "I may have more years behind me than up ahead," she said, "but I don't have a dim view of the future. There is still plenty of time ahead for good living and for enjoying my own lovely things. Eventually I will give them to my children and grandchildren. I have labeled the furniture, the paintings and my needlepoint. I labeled my jewelry, too. I wrote the name of the one who admired it most and who will cherish it. Someday it will be theirs. Occasional hints are dropped. I hear them, but I don't mind. I'm amused. I can afford to be. At my age it's part of life to plan ahead."

When grandchildren first pick up their gift-wrapped presents, grandmothers start thinking about *grand openings*. The excitement builds if she and the grandchildren can spend time speculating, "Whatever can it be?"

No matter how expensive or inexpensive the gift, we are delighted when our grandchildren show us they like and appreciate our present. We plunge into miserable despair when they don't. The *coup de grace* comes when a gift that was lovingly chosen is tossed aside with a hurried, "Thank you." Deprived of the child's anticipated gasps of pleasure, we struggle with the tightening in our throat and tears that blur our vision. My God! All that time shopping—all that tissue paper—the special ribbon rosette! And what about the card selected after reading dozens of other cards? We watch in tense silence as the card and wrapping are crumpled. Children are not taught these days to save gift wrappings.

But even these feelings pale when compared with what we experience when a gift-wrapped package is acknowledged with a casual shrug and left unopened.

We don't expect declarations of gratitude. We don't need them. But a present specially packaged for a child means the unwrapping is fun for Grandma, too. She looks forward to it. Why deprive her of the fun? After all, how many games can a grandmother play without getting winded?

When little children don't give a big hurrah for a present they get, we can still smile understandingly and say, "They're only children." When their parents fail to give an enthusiastic response to a present *they* get, one to which we gave considerable thought and time, we might resort to some daring tactics.

"Why carry the burden of smoldering hurt?" Vera asked. "When my son and daughter-in-law tossed off another careless, 'Thanks a lot Mom, we'll open it later,' that seemed callous to me. I stared at the beautifully gift-wrapped package, remembering how I had watched to make sure the store clerk didn't skimp on the colored tissue paper. I gathered courage that moment and drew upon my sense of humor. On their anniversary, I brought over a large package wrapped in brown paper and tied with string. In bilious green, my son's most unfavorite color, I wrote: 'Dear Ones, this is for your room, a special thought for your anniversary. Love, Mother.'

"Both the present and I were impossible to ignore, right there in the middle of the room. They could not avoid opening the package. My daughter-in-law gingerly removed the stiff, recycled paper with a quizzical expression. I think she was already suspicious. I watched as an enlarged photograph of myself wearing a mink coat, long earrings and a benign smile was revealed, all in an ornate gilded frame.

"The effect was electrifying! Marvelous! Their faces turned white, then flushed red. I beamed and look beneficently at them. 'Ha ha,' my son said bravely, 'you *are* a cute practical joker, Mom!' He continued cautiously, 'We wanted an antique map for the fireplace and you present us with your portrait. Mom, you're wonderful!' My daughter-in-law seemed transfixed. But I had accomplished my purpose. I got the hurt off my chest. My family knows how much I enjoy giving presents. I made my point. No need to hammer it in. We all had a good laugh. They got their antique map. The mills of the gods grind slowly but exceedingly fine."

Giving gifts is not a one-way street. Grandmothers get presents, too. Some tend to shriek with glee, forced or real, when they open a present. "Just what I wanted!" they cry. Other grandmothers tone down the shouts. Some specialize in a particular grandmotherly smile and a slightly tearful, "Thank you, darlings." Other grandmothers hardly respond at all.

"I know a grandmother who reacts to a present as if it's a time bomb or germ-laden," a doctor said. "She asks the giver to open the wrapping. She looks at the contents from a safe distance, with her head stiffly tilted back. After a moment's glance, she grants a tight little 'Thank you very much.' My own mother-in-law begins with, 'Although I appreciate the thought, I'll have very little use for something like that. Give it to somebody who can use it, or bring it back and ask them to return your money. Thanks anyway.'"

Two types of presents give grandmothers special pleasure. If a gift screams *expensive*, the grandmother's neighbors and friends are sure to notice it. They will want to talk about it, and the grandmother can then brag about who gave it to her. Another wonderful type of gift is something the grandmother couldn't afford or would have hesitated to buy for herself. Such extravagant, thoughtful presents are deeply appreciated.

8
Paper Bridges

Letters are precious lifelines between grandmother and the family. They can triumph over any distance. They sometimes are the only connection people have. Separations are painful enough. Loneliness and longing become bearable when a letter arrives that is warm and understanding, carrying family news, a bit of gossip, something to smile about, something to feel grateful for.

Letters are paper bridges. Their words are sounds that otherwise might never be heard. A grandmother just doesn't read a letter. She absorbs it. The best letters arrive in a steady flow at just the right time with just the right thoughts. A grandmother frequently holds a letter tenderly before opening it, reliving certain moments.

Grandmothers are letter-savers. They tie them in ribbons, put them away in boxes, tuck them in drawers. A grandmother can spend a day re-reading a packet of letters. Without them, she may find her days are filled with unending solitude.

Pity the grandmother whose mailbox is empty day after day. As her friends produce sheaves of letters, postcards and family announcements, she smiles bravely. She is happy for the other grandmothers who are sharing their joy. She understands. But when she is alone after having faced the empty mailbox again, the thought of being overlooked sends tears sliding down her cheeks.

Never mind the scrawl, brevity or fumbling for words, she prays. Just let me receive a letter from a loved one in my mailbox, rather than another advertisement for a new detergent.

Dear Pop Pop and Grandma Edith,

Sorry I took so long to write. A couple of weeks ago I started studying to play the violin and the drums. Now I can play violin, electric guitar, drums and piano. I am playing "Yellow Submarine" and "Blue Moon" in my school concert. Yesterday I fell off my bicycle and went to the hospital. I have 40 stitches in my chin, two chipped teeth, many scratches and bad bruises on my hands, arms and stomach. My daddy is working hard and all the time. How are you feeling? Write soon. I am typing this letter on the computer.

Love,
Mitchell

Dear Granny and Grandfather,

This is the second time I am writing this day. I am dieting. Don't worry. Your aloud to eat whenever you want at camp. Please send cheese and crackers and also candy. I am not a spoiled bratt. Like I said you don't have to. Well you know something? You better bring it next visiting day.

I love you,
Julie

Dear Grandma,

I like camp very much. I raced against two girls and one was a year older than me. I won them. I have a soar throat and a ear acke but it is going away. I am going to tell you the rest when I get home. You know. The secrets. o.k.?

Hugs and kisses,
Susan

June 2

Risa darling,

I know what you are going through. Don't worry, dear. You'll get your period. Already you are wearing a "B" cup. That's a good sign. Wait. It will come. It always does. Believe me.

Lovingly,
Grandmother
G-m-r

July 15

Dear Grandma,

I got it! I got it! I'm so happy now. It happened just like you promised. Grandma, I love you.

Risa

143

Andrea Darling,

I'm glad you can pour out your little heart to Grandma. Of course I understand. Of course I'll help. Don't be upset, sweetheart. It has happened before to plenty of girls. Just don't tell your mother or daddy until I prepare them. Parents don't appreciate such surprises. Bring the young man to me first. We will have a nice talk. Then you can tell your parents. They will understand. It can be a small, quiet wedding, but soon! That way it won't interfere with your studies. You'll manage the wedding, the baby and the master's degree in time.

Lovingly,
Grandma

My dear Lillian,

Do I have to tell you how good it is to hear from an old, dear friend? I wish you didn't live so far away. I'm happy you enjoy your grandchildren. Mine are also wonderful. My oldest grandson sometimes stays with me over a weekend. He brings his bedmate. She is a nice, quiet girl with sandals, blue beads, long wavy hair and thin braids all around her head. She plays the guitar.

Last Sunday I went to religious services. I have a good relationship with our spiritual leader. He calls me by my first name. Lillian dear, take care of yourself.

Love,
Martha

Dear Grandma,

Alice and I have decided to separate barring a last-minute change of heart. We wanted you to get the sad news directly from us rather than from others. Alice will have custody of Jamie and will be living about 50 miles away, so I will be able to see him quite often. I'll try to make sure that you get to see him, too. Alice and I both want him to know his grandmother. Alice has already started to look at apartments. She may well move out within a few weeks. We both feel sad and a little scared about the change, but living together has been hellish for both of us for about 10 months. Neither of us sees much prospect for improvement. Whether the separation will lead to divorce isn't entirely clear. I feel that at least for me, it will help clarify my feelings. Thanks for being so close to us and for the cute outfit you sent. It's just the right size for him now. He is, as you might imagine, very cute. He's crawling around quite deftly and has become more responsive and aware. Naturally, I feel badly about him not living with me, but I also feel that two parents painfully at odds with one another are not the kinds of role models I want for him. There's lots more to tell, of course, but I'll save it until we get together. Meanwhile, I'm sending on some new photos of Jamie.

Love,
Dennis

Dear Dennis,

I am sorry that you and Alice are having serious problems. Perhaps she is unhappy because you have to travel so much and she is alone so often. I hope the situation takes a turn for the better. You and Alice can be sure I will always feel that Jamie is very precious to me.

I send all of you my love,
Grandmother

September 16

Dearest Vera,

I'm feeling so upset and blue. Nothing helps. I can't help feeling left out in the family. I guess I need a miracle. I've tried everything: the cakes, the suppers, presents, baby-sitting, telephoning every day, bringing food coupons I could use myself. I even try to look especially nice so they will be proud of me. Vera, you won't believe what I'm going to tell you, but so help me God, it's true. My children talk in some foreign language in front of me so I won't understand what they are saying. What can I do? I try not to complain. But I'm only human and I'm still mourning my husband. Sometimes a sigh escapes from my heart. I bear it and don't say a word. I'm sorry to write such a sad letter.

Love,
Regina

September 25

Dear Regina,

Stop with the dinners and telephone calls! You are doing entirely the wrong thing. What happened to you? You used to be so smart! If you are there, you are in the way. If you are not there, you are not in the way. In fact, you may even be missed. Try my approach. My children run after me with, "Mother dear, we're missing you." Avoid them a little. Learn from your mistakes. Be smart. It works. Did you know Tillie joined the Ladies Sports Activity Club and pulled her shoulder out of place? She's in the hospital. I think she would appreciate a visit. Bring those dinners to her!

Love,
Vera

Dear Mother,

You're in Florida. I'm in New York. When I tell you the news you'll be on top of the world. Be calm. You are about to become a grandmother again and a great grandmother, too! Your granddaughter Carol is in her fifth month and your daughter Connie (me) is in the fourth!

When Carol said she was pregnant again, I said, "Carol, how could you?" She said, "It's so easy, Mommy. You should know!" I bet you can't wait to tell your girlfriends. Keep well. Save your strength. We're depending on you.

Lovingly,
Connie

Dear Ones,

Received your letter yesterday. I mailed one a few days ago. As usual, our letters crossed. I've had a spell of loneliness. I'm one of those people who likes people and can't be alone too much. If not for the pain in my legs and arms, I would help out at a hospital. I still do things for charity when I can. I write what I feel because I know you understand. My apartment can be like a jail. There are times when I'm happiest in it anyway. I always say if you can't get it in bushels, take it by spoonfuls. Lots of love to you and the children. Keep writing.

Grandmother Edna

Dear Children,

I just can't figure you out. It's enough to make me crazy. First you plan to visit and be with the family. No outside business. The next thing I hear, you're going on a trip to Switzerland. I never tell my children what to do. I know there are reasons. Do what's best for you. I'll be here. You're always more than welcome. We think about you all the time. Love from Dad and me. Have a good time.

Mom

Dear Sarah,

Well, it's over! What a wedding! It was hard to tell who belonged to whom. I held my great-grandson while his parents stood under the wedding canopy. Listen, he's a fine young man. He loves my granddaughter. She's pregnant again, which is why they are getting married.

So that's the story. Now you know why I didn't get to your grandson's bar mitzvah. The couple went on a honeymoon. I'm there, too, with the baby. A real family affair. It's very complicated. Regards.

Your friend,
Minnie

Dear Frances and Joe,

Just a short letter to let you know I'm not going. The vacation is off. I slipped and I broke my wrist in several places. I'll be in a cast for six weeks. Don't get excited. Otherwise I'm fine. The weather is terrible. Mostly cold, wind, rain. When the cast comes off, I'll need physiotherapy. God was good to me. It could have been worse.

Love to all,
Mamma

Dear Marcia,

The time has come to tell you I'm leaving your father (for a while, anyway). I've had it. After 37 years of wedlock, we've arrived at a deadlock. He can take care of himself and some other things he's been taking for granted. He's a good man and still your father. Don't think differently about him because of me.

No need to tell me to see a marriage counselor or a shrink. I could teach THEM a few things. You gave me books to read on women's equality and assertiveness. They made sense.

I gave your father the best years of my life. According to those books, I have more years ahead than I realized for self-actualization. Tell my darling grandchildren Grandma is having a nice rest.

I'll be staying with my closest friend (you know who). I saved money for a rainy day. It's pouring now. It's time to use my umbrella. Look in and see how your father is getting along.

Love,
Mother

P.S. The receipt for the dry cleaner and the telephone bill are in the kitchen closet, middle shelf, right-hand side.

Dear Eunice and Albert,

I'm home. I know you're surprised. I was sick when I went to the hotel and sick when I was there. The food was awful, and such small portions. Two miserable weeks. Even the weather. The people weren't friendly. Now that I'm home I feel better. I'll manage. I'm taking life as it comes. Be well. If you feel like visiting, I'm here. God bless.

Grandma Liz

Dear Catherine,

How are you, my dear? I thought you'd like to know I am keeping quite well. I did see that nice young doctor I told you about. I remembered to bring the list of my problems written on a sheet of paper. It's hard to remember and tell a doctor everything. It's just possible to overlook an important symptom. The young doctor examined me and said there was little he could do except to say that for my age, I am indeed well and should not expect more. Well! I was not pleased with his frankness. I told him, "Young man, I knew your father, who was also our doctor for many years. I even remember the day you were born. I am going to teach you a lesson today. Never tell a woman of my age that she should not expect more. Shame on you! Your father would never have said that, not in a million years. And don't bother to send a bill. I just gave you a lesson." With that I marched out of his office. Just thought I'd bring you up to date. And so it goes.

Love,
Beatrice

9
Family Feelings

Harmony Cookies

1 cup love
2 tablespoons criticism
1 pinch sarcasm
1 tablespoon sweetener
1 cup sifted animosity
1-1/2 cups patience
1-1/2 cups sympathy

Blend ingredients. Bake at warm temperature. Do not slam doors while cookies are baking. While still warm, sprinkle with good humor and sugar. Serve in large portions.

People say family feelings aren't what they used to be. Distance and the pace of modern life are straining family ties. People make sporadic forays back into the family circle for traditional or obligatory occasions. Other than that, everyone follows his or her own path.

But family feelings are remarkably deep-seated and can be renewed surprisingly easily. Someone always seems to be able to pick up a dangling thread from a relationship and weave it back into the family tapestry.

Grandmothers are great catalysts for bringing families together. They are treasure houses of miscellaneous information that fascinate and tantalize. They usually are at their talkative best when revealing family history—skeletons and all. Memories of the past grow sharper with age, and grandmothers know how to make history colorful. But, they also are discreet, careful not to hurt anyone's feelings.

Grandmothers are natural arbitrators of family disputes. They have inherent abilities as psychologists, negotiators, mentors and healers. Whether a grandmother is a mountain of strength or petite and fragile, she has an aura of wisdom and authority. Grandmothers strive to protect the family's reputation and to soothe ruffled feelings. They go to great pains to avoid wrecking the outside world's illusions that their families are "ideal."

Crisis Intervention—Grandmother Style

Not long ago, family life was centered, connected and dutifully attended to. It was filled with small pleasures. But things have changed in the last 20 years. With the rise of divorce and single parenting, a grandmother's door may be the only one open when marriages fall apart or a family crisis occurs.

Frankly, as a grandmother, I don't feel answerable to my children. But it's hard to ignore grandchildren. Here I am, like old times, working away again in the kitchen. It's not easy, but I love those kids. They are sweet. I had to drop out of the course I was hooked on—the one on ethnic folklore. The aerobic exercise class is out of the question now. I settled for a Jane Fonda tape. I'm needed. I'm here. Whatever. That son-in-law of mine dropped out of sight. My poor daughter is looking for a job. And what other things would a grandmother rather be doing at a time like this, anyway?

Rebecca W.

Very little escapes a grandmother's notice. She recognizes swallowed resentments and injured pride. She is no stranger to undercurrents of jealousy, anger and emotional pain. She has her own kind of courage and will tell the family what it does not always want to hear. Although this may make her temporarily unpopular, she isn't surprised and can handle it. After all, she has accumulated considerable experience as a mother and mother-in-law.

Many times, Grandma forces the family to accept its responsibilities. Smiling bravely, she enters the arena, makes a statement and leaves before her intervention can be labeled *interference.*

If a falling-out between family members cannot be resolved, it can break Grandma's heart. Heartbreak heals slowly, if at all.

When the world turns its back or someone in the family needs help, Grandma rallies the family together.

What family doesn't have some kind of trouble? How wonderful it is to have the comfort of a grandmother's soothing words and wisdom, rather than having to turn to mere acquaintances who feed on others' misery. Many people mistakenly fear that family feelings will fence them in, that family members will expect too much of them. Perhaps that is why some grandmothers and children are left alone so much of the time!

In any case, don't worry. Family feelings are still there. It may take more these days to get people to acknowledge and respond to these feelings. But once they do, the family can accomplish anything. Somehow, when one member falls to the depths or stumbles into a maze of bad times, the others help that person find a way out.

"What amazes me," May said, "is how tightly woven we all are at the roots. How strong the roots are, and how deep they go into the past."

Who Did It to Whom?

Mom-Blamers are self-styled experts who trace back with insatiable vengeance the ways in which mothers (and therefore grandmothers) ruined or emotionally crippled their children. Many of us would like to know where they got their information.

Mom-Blaming has gone beyond reasonable limits. I am not even sure what it is I am being blamed for. The accusations run the gamut. They include MY responsibility for THEIR inability to establish enduring relationships with the opposite sex, failure to achieve full orgasmic potential and an inability to change their miserable dispositions. I am also blamed for their impossible eating habits, fears, phobias, laziness, bossiness and allergies. I, for one, am stunned and can only stammer, "Who, me?"

As a mother and grandmother, I don't accept those stabs in the back, those slurs and undeserved innuendoes. Nor do I crumble into little bits and pieces. Why construe what I may have done wrongly or ineptly in the past as a fatal blunder? Of course there were some bungles and foul-ups, but who needs to be reminded? No mother wants to be told that what she did "way back when" was wrong. Grandmothers believe that everything done with LOVE must perforce be right.

Hannah R.

165

What Is, Is!

The past is past. What is, is. I have learned to love and to forgive myself and others. If some memories jar my self-esteem, why burden myself with them? Sometimes it hurts and is done with anguish. But I don't want to feel bitterness. Nor do I want to blame or hurt another.

Mildred T.

My Daughters' Husbands

My son-in-law can be a pride and joy, the kind I think of as a son. He wants the grandchildren to know me and to appreciate having a grandmother. He brings me, takes me, opens the car door and doesn't hug me only in public. He even calls from his office without being reminded, and is pleased that my daughter resembles me more every year. He enjoys my house, raves about my cooking and brings presents. When I tell the neighbors about my daughter's husband, they drool with envy.

My other son-in-law is the easygoing type. I visit them in the country. My daughter complained for years about a large crack in the floor of the garage. I bought the proper mixture, put a mat under my knees and one afternoon began to fill the crack with new cement. My son-in-law and little grandson walked into the garage, stepped over me and the pail and said, "Hi, Grandma." Then they both walked out. I guess there's nothing unusual about a grandmother doing a little cement work.

Anna W.

My Son's Wife

How does one learn to be a good mother-in-law and a good grandmother? The experts say a daughter-in-law tends to take a mother-in-law for granted. The reverse doesn't seem to hold true.

"Personally, my son's wife is the same as a daughter to me—occasionally. When she has a meeting and asks me to pick up the children at school and get a few bottles of milk and some odds and ends at the supermarket, I may feel like a shop-and-deliver service, but I do it. After all, a grandmother is supposed to..."

Sometimes a daughter-in-law thinks you have nothing important to do anyway, or assumes that helping her is what you've been waiting to do all your life. But other times, a daughter-in-law says, "Mother dear, do what is best for you. Think of yourself for a change."

Sometimes when a daughter-in-law is angry or silent, it has nothing to do with you. It is a sign that the marriage is in trouble, or that her husband is neglecting her. At other times, a daughter-in-law may become angry at something a mother-in-law has done, and then may stay angry so long it becomes a habit. She may have bad feelings long after both she and you have forgotten what originally angered her in the first place. Sometimes you find yourself saying, "Never again! I won't take it." But you do, because you miss the grandchildren, your son looks tired or she's really a good mother. And sometimes you may also think that any girl who can live with your son deserves a lot of credit!

My other son's wife is studying interior decorating. She's sweet and likes to be helpful. When she visits, the furniture gets moved around.

Just when I would enjoy a sit-down with my feet up, and a nice chat over a cup of coffee, she gets busy. Maybe she thinks we don't have anything to talk about. Or maybe because she knows she can't change me, it's her way of changing something about me.

I know the signs. She looks a bit restless and begins with, "Mother dear, y'know what I think?" Her voice trails off as she surveys the room. It's her profession, so I let her get it out of her system. Everything is put back where it was when she leaves, anyway.

The marble statue of Beatrice on the pedestal in the living room is my favorite possession. Each morning I look at her serene smile and say, "Good morning, Beatrice." It's a nice way to start the day. But one time my daughter-in-law moved her to a hallway corner. What a backbreaking job it was moving her back to her old location! I wouldn't hurt the feelings of my daughter-in-law for the world. But now I have one rule. No changing the scenery when I'm not at home. No surprises, please!

Ethel R.

Double Messages from Grandmother

They never come to see me.

It's wonderful when they come and better when they go.

I have nothing to look forward to.

Thanks for the invitation, but I don't like to be locked in to long-range plans.

I thought I knew a few things.

Why always ask me? Am I supposed to know all the answers?

I'm no longer consulted.

No one listens anyway.

Whatever happened to family feelings?

Why come to me when there's trouble?

I have an open mind.

I'm used to doing things my way.

Why not ask *me* to do it?

I'm always being put upon.

Who says I'm not willing and able?

I haven't the same energy I used to have.

You can depend on me to be truthful.

There's so much to say, but my lips are sealed.

You're looking well.

Have you been to a doctor lately?

Getting Even

> *I make them anxious, even worry them a little. I just don't answer the phone early in the morning or late in the evening, when they are sure I'm home. They haven't called me for several days; why should they take me for granted? When they ask, "How are you?" I wait a long moment, sigh and say, "Don't worry, I'll manage."*
>
> Katie W.

> *I pull out my dentures and show them where my gums hurt.*
>
> Bess L.

The experts tell us it is important to let off steam and to clear the air. They say, "Tell the family they made you angry and why. Tell them when they hurt your feelings, and when you think you are misunderstood. Give them a piece of your mind. Don't let them get away with it."

A grandmother will tell you from personal experience that such advice is rubbish! Most of the time getting angry raises your blood pressure, creates bad feelings and makes someone feel guilty. Showing anger is counterproductive, and in the end, anger can make the situation worse, not better. Grandmothers are experts about anger. They have had plenty of experience deciding when to keep their lips sealed and when to open them.

Sometimes, however, emotions just spill over. A grandmother's feelings may be so strong that she can't help but reveal them. She often regrets this later. She gets tangled in webs she never meant to spin. Anger is an intense, transitory emotion that should be diffused, not intensified. Wisdom dictates that when a grandmother begins feeling anger building, she should remove herself from the situation, if only for a few moments. She should divert her mind and think of something to smile about. Some grannies practice deep-breathing exercises. They let feelings of tranquillity flow through them, then go back to business as usual.

I tell them I met an old friend who said, "I didn't know you were alive. I was afraid to ask your family, because I don't see you with them anymore."

Nina F.

I don't really want to be mean, but when my family starts talking about their problems, I stop them short and say, "You didn't come to me then, why ask me now?"

Jessie P.

When they say "Good morning" to me, I say, "What's so good about it?"

Sylvia S.

When they tell me in detail about the theater, concert or ballet they enjoyed, I remind them that I used to take THEM and that maybe now it is time to take ME.

Daisy K.

When they begin to look around my house at my treasures with undisguised intent, as if they are taking inventory, I say, "Don't worry my darlings, I know who wants what."

Selma J.

When they are watching TV, I come up with a reminder that I'll be needing a refill of Geritol and Maalox.

Audrey H.

Sometimes they don't bother with a gift, even on a special occasion. I mention by-the-by, "My friend, Celia, wears a diamond brooch her children gave her without an occasion. But who needs to be a target for a mugging?"

Jenny G.

I tell my children, "If I had my life to live over again, I wouldn't have children." But I'm glad I have children to say it to.

Therese P.

It's Not an Insult If Your Grandchildren Ask . . .

When you die will you leave me money if there's any left?

Why do you have wrinkles and brown spots?

When you were little, were you on the North or the South side in the Civil War?

When you were a girl, did you have a bathroom? Were you *very* poor? No car? No radio, either? Did you have a stove? You didn't have television!

It's Not an Insult When . . .

They prefer watching TV when you're there.
They don't write thank-you notes or greeting cards.
They don't call.
They no longer like the sweets you carry in your handbag.
They answer the telephone and say, "What do you want, Grandma? I'm watching television."
They suddenly dump the standards you thought were *eternal*.

Grandma Is Coming to Our House!

Some grandmothers enter like a tornado.
Some creep in like a mouse.
Others twitter like a sparrow,
Or fall exhausted on the nearest couch.

Planning to just pop in, are we? Phone first and ring the doorbell when you get there.

10
Listen to Us, Grandma!

Glossary for Grandmothers

Babies—Angels whose wings get smaller as their legs grow longer.
Beautiful!—We agree on that!
Blast—The absolute greatest fun!
Boo-boo—Anything from a scratch to a need for love.
Cool it—Calm down, let it pass, no sweat.
Dynamite—It's super, colossal.
Gross—Ugh! (Also see yucky.)
I gotta make—Head for the nearest bathroom.
Let's share—I want what you have, but I'm not giving you what I have.
Neat—Couldn't be nicer. I like it.
No way—Forget it! You're getting nowhere.
Right on—It's OK.
The pits—The absolute lowest.
Vibes—You're getting through to me.
You're a dum-dum—I'm angry at you.
You're nice—What did you bring for me?
Yucky—Unpleasant. Check your breath, armpits and feet.

Letters to Grandma

When we ask for snacks, you say it's not healthy, you'll get diarrhea, it will ruin your teeth, it's too soon before dinner. Aw, quit it, Grandma!

Billy, age 9

You ask the same questions all the time. "How is school? What is your teacher's name? How was your report card? Are you a good girl?" Grandma, a GOOD question would be, "What do you want for a present?"

Julie, age 7

In school today, the teacher told us about a poet who walked all alone in the woods. He listened to the birds, he looked at the sky, he looked at the trees, he looked at the flowers. There was nobody to "noodgie" him, so don't "noodgie" me.

Mattie, age 5

You always say, "I just had the cleaning girl and it cost a fortune. Don't touch the furniture. Don't walk on the rug. I haven't the strength to vacuum footprints or crumbs." Grandma, where are we supposed to go?

Richard, age 11

Grandma, I don't want to sleep in your bed. You snore. And please don't leave your teeth smiling in the glass.

Dorothy, age 12

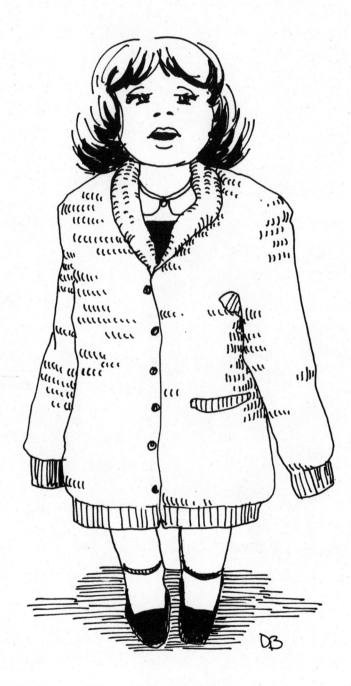

Grandmother dear, I know you love me, but stop trying to fatten me up. I SAW you pouring cream into the milk when you thought I wasn't looking.

Susan, age 14

Nana, why do my clothes bother you so much? You always have something to say about my hair. What's SO important about shoes? And, Nana, boys DO wear beads.

Andy, age 16

Granny, don't set your heart on my being a doctor. Acting IS a good profession, and don't say, "GOD FORBID!"

Larry, age 18

Grandma, please don't say nasty things about certain relatives I happen to like. I know by heart how you gave the best years of your life to the family. And please, Grandma, don't complain about Grandpa to me. I love him very much.

Edith, age 16

I know you love to knit, but please make it to fit this time.

Stephanie, age 18

Don't ask me again, Grandma. Believe me, you'll be the first to know if I'm getting married.

Michelle, age 30

Kid Bits

Jackie: Grandma, I know where babies come from.
Grandma: Tell me, darling.
Jackie: Babies come from Daddy's seeds.
Grandma: Where are the seeds, dear?
Jackie: In the garage, where he keeps things for the garden.

Donald: Granny, I'm going to marry Susan.
Grandma: She's only 9 years old. How will you take care of her?
Donald: Oh, that's easy. I'll work and get money.
Grandma: But what if you have children?
Donald: Well, we've been lucky so far.

Marjorie: Mommy, where is the new baby?
Mommy: In my uterus.
Marjorie: Take it out and show it to me!

Kathleen: Grandma, how were babies born a thousand years ago?
Grandma: Naked, darling.

Susan: Which is the wiser bird, Grandma, the owl or the stork?
Grandma: The stork, dear. The owl only says, "Who." The stork *knows* who.

About My Grandmothers

I have two grandmothers. One is my visiting grandmother, who lives quite far away and gets on a train to visit us. She always looks very dressed up. She belongs to Daddy. My other grandmother lives with us in our house. She belongs to Mommy and is very little.

When visiting grandmother eats, she chews a long time and touches her mouth with a napkin. Once I counted 23 touches. She hardly ever talks while she's eating except to say, "Good morning" or "Please pass the sugar" or "Would you mind pouring a little water for Grandmother, dear?" Sometimes she speaks to Mommy in French because Mommy knows French. They say things in French I don't understand. Mommy said Daddy's Mom lived in Paris and is an elegant lady. I asked Mommy, "Why do you get up early to make special things for visiting grandmother's breakfast that you don't make for us?" She said, "Because first, she's a grandmother; second, she's Daddy's mother; and third, that's the way grandmothers should be treated—special! And someday you will understand."

When visiting grandmother gets off the train, she carries a small valise, a big pocketbook and a box of chocolates for the family. She always wears gloves. I kiss her and we all get into the car. I look up at her and smile. She smiles down and pats my hand. When we get to the house I ask her if she brought the "you know what." She nods her head and says, "Yes, dear, always. It is inside the valise." She opens it very carefully with a small key.

"Look!" she says, taking out the white linen envelope with the beautiful, lacy edge. Inside is the little prayer book and white handkerchief with three initials in the corner. Visiting grandmother puts the prayer book gently on the handkerchief. Then she fixes her eyeglasses on her face. Her lips talk, but I don't understand the words. She says, "I am praying, and this is how God and I talk things over together."

After dinner, visiting grandmother sits in Daddy's special chair. Nobody dares to tell her it's Daddy's chair, least of all Daddy. She sits there looking at us very pleased, and smiles as if she thinks we are having only nice thoughts about her.

One morning, very early, Mommy and I heard noises and peeked into visiting grandmother's room. She was on the floor doing strong exercises, "One, two, three," and so on. Mommy looked at me and her eyes were very big. "Hmmm," she said, "and I thought she was so weak."

When visiting grandmother leaves, we give each other kisses again. She looks soft and pretty, but when she holds me close, she feels like a stick. Even so, I really love her. Mommy said that visiting grandmother had a sad life with many troubles. You can tell, because she gnashes her teeth when she sleeps.

My other grandmother is sweet and funny. She's always poking in the refrigerator, or is at the sink washing dishes, peeling potatoes or knitting. She still holds me on her lap (although I'm quite big now). She brushes and braids my hair, mends my clothes and helps sew dolls' dresses. She lets me dance for her until I want to stop. No one else listens to my make-believe stories and tells me there is nothing else in the whole world she would rather be doing.

When my little grandmother has her arthritis, she calls it "Arthur." "Arthur is here again," she sighs. Daddy helps her up and down, takes her to the doctor and hugs her a lot. He is so kind. I asked him why he loves little grandmother so much. He said, "First, she's a grandmother; second, she's Mommy's mother; third, that is the way grandmothers should be treated—special! And someday you will understand."

Daphne, age 10

Grandma, Stop It!

Grandmother dear, must you be so curious and gregarious when my friends are around? Must you always make some statement or comment that breaks with traditional grandmotherly behavior? I appreciate your ultramodern attitudes, but your postscripts are something else. Please don't EVER tell my friends that our family is like a "stagnant bureaucracy" or that "when a girl likes, she lets, and when she loves, she helps." And wherever did you get THAT one from?

Laura, age 19

I know you weren't born yesterday, Grandma, and that you know a lot about sex. You have definite guidelines, rules of thumb and no-nos related to unmarried girls, brides, pregnant women and so on. There isn't a single problem you can't deal with on these subjects. The only hitch, Grandma, is that you never give a straight answer. All I get are detours around the subject.

Elizabeth, age 17

When you and I are having a nice little chat together, Grandma, why must you bring up the subject of my not wanting to live at home? My mind is made up. Please don't spend good energy on useless arguments and trying to solve all the world's problems. Save your strength for vital changes and your own needs. As a future psychologist, I must caution you not to drain your reservoirs of energies. Please, Grandmother. Don't be angry with me, but really, sometimes you express a sense of mission bordering on the messianic. Mother says I take after you.

Adrienne, age 24

198

Sometimes I don't understand why you turn off the ones you want to be closest to. You tell us you can not wait to die. Then you worry like crazy that some lunatic will see to it that you do. You run to the doctor and then come back feeling that he wasn't interested or competent because he didn't specify a date of demise. Grandma, why do you do this to us?

Gloria, age 25

It is very interesting to know for the millionth time that your own mother, who was my great-grandmother, lived to the ripe old age of 97. It's also nice to know that she kept a record of family events, births, deaths, and the dates and nature of her surgical operations, including names of doctors and fees. It's boring to be told over and over that she ate all the "right" foods. Well, Grandma, I like large steaks and beer, and LOATHE keeping lists and records. This apple fell far from the tree because it was on a steep hill. Just love me as I am. OK?

Barbara, age 18

Don't look so shocked, Grandma. Why not face the facts? Keep yourself informed and up-to-date. Every woman should know her own cervix. I'm giving you disposable plastic speculums and a mirror. Women don't have to visit a male gynecologist for every little problem. I'm also giving you the telephone number of the Women's Information Center for the name of the nearest female gynecologist. (Or see my doctor, she's excellent.)

Diane, age 22

Betty Friedan's book, *The Feminine Mystique*, struck a deep emotional chord in many women. Daughters, wives, mums and grannies realized that perhaps they *had* been undervalued. Perhaps they *had* been overly accepting. "Keep her pregnant and barefoot in the kitchen," men said, laughing. But you better believe they meant it. The initial reaction of some feminists seemed a bit excessive. But the movement needed that push to get off the ground.

Another bit of nonsense that passed for truth was that a woman's virtue was between her legs. Well, Betty Friedan, Gloria Steinem, Germaine Greer, Alice Walker and others helped women get a different perspective on their sexuality. They mince no words as they pursue the feminist crusade with courage.

Now even grannies feel less ashamed about their erotic fantasies. So what if Grandma imagines herself looking like Greer Garson, sipping sherry with Cary Grant at 2 in the afternoon, with "I've Got You Under My Skin" playing softly in the background? Grandmothers are taking another look at their urges and reconsidering some prevailing notions about their lifestyles. If grannies are the basis of family legends, why shouldn't they make their lives more interesting? The feminist movement is revitalizing grandmothers by showing them how to turn ideas into experience.

I joined the feminist movement, and have a membership card for NOW (National Organization for Women). For the first time in my life I have a T-shirt with the feminist symbol across the front. I bought one for my daughter and granddaughter. My daughter went a little too far, however, when she gave me a T-shirt with the slogan, "I love my body, but I share." (She got carried away by her own enthusiasm.) At my advanced age, this was to let me know that perhaps I still had cards of my own to play.

Irma G.

I was enthusiastic about the things the women's movement was doing. I could see clearly the defensive vindictiveness with which some men attacked the feminists. But there were also many men who sympathized with the feminists' cause; men who appreciated these women and were not afraid to come right out and say it. Of course, they were at a disadvantage. Many feminists said, "Thanks, but it sounds condescending. We don't need bolstering comments to give us validation. Show us action! Forget about the utterances. We're not on a warpath. We're blazing new trails and you're welcome to join us if you can keep up with the pace."

Nicole Y.

I'm a grandmother. I like the ideas about freedom and certain rights. Suddenly, men don't seem so superior anymore. The problem for me is that my enthusiasm usually fades away as soon as I open the front door. Sure, I approve. So why do I find it so hard to change? I suppose there's something ingrained in my character from way back. Inwardly I've changed. Outwardly? No. I seem to be the same as I ever was. I intend to continue my membership dues and read feminist books. I can't promise anything else. I'll say what my grandmother said: "Well, God, if you can't change me, please, just use me as I am."

Mabel E.

I think these modern women have gone too far. They will regret it. Some of them are thoroughly disrespectful toward men. I know lots of men who have patience and are real nice. They have a way with children. They do their share and don't leave all the work to the women, as the women's movement says they do. But to tell the truth, my father was a man I feared and respected. "Women are in the world to have children and bring them up. Men are in the world to run it and fix things." That's what Papa always said, and wouldn't he just turn in his grave if he knew that plenty of women read the stock reports and run a business?

Alice O.

A grandmother who knows how to rap with her grandchildren about the pill and issues such as substance abuse is on the right road. It doesn't mean compromising values and morality. It's a compliment when a daughter or granddaughter shares a woman-to-woman secret.

I Love You "10," Grandma, And That's All the Way

You are an important person in the family,
Someone we treasure, the link between.
A source of inheritance (but don't take it wrongly).
In the stories and songs only you remember,
The roots of tradition rub off like indelible ink.
You love me.
And I know it.
On a scale from 1 to 10, I love you "10," Grandma.

Your house is unchanged, familiar and warm,
With goodies in the same little drawer
Where I can always find them,
As if you know I am coming, or hope I will.
Everything tastes better when you make it
And I eat it in your house.
I tell you things I don't tell others,
And tell others things I don't tell you.
You read me like a book.
On a scale from 1 to 10, I love you "10," Grandma.

You are romantic, sentimental, and by golly,
You have rhythm.
I saw you dancing by yourself to music from the radio.
Practical Grandma! Provident and extravagant!
Inclined to give us expensive gifts.
At family parties you can dazzle with your wit.
Sometimes you sit alone and apart,
With thoughts too far for me to reach.
On a scale from 1 to 10, I love you "10," Grandma.

You are a little fussy and can be contentious,
But you never complain or regret.
When I speak, you listen and question with your talking eyes.
I don't know how you manage to be stoic and saintly.
You smell delicious, sweet soapy clean
(But sometimes like camphor, antiseptic).
And when you say it will be all right, Grandma,
It will be.
(Even if you have to talk
To my parents to make it so.)
On a scale from 1 to 10, I love you "10," Grandma!

Dolly, age 18

Thank You

Darling Nan, when I long for the sound of your voice,
The closeness of your presence,
I run to you with some flimsy excuse.
But I'm not always at home in your bustling house;
Words and unfamiliar sounds fall around me
Like pebbles and stones.
Suddenly, I long for the quiet of my dry-leaf world,
But thank you for letting me weep or laugh
Without feeling ashamed,
For your closeness when the world seems unfriendly
Or life a bit frightening.
For breaking the silence of miles and hours,
And for your honest eyes when they read my face.

Grandma Edna (Nana)

Come to Me

Come to me, Grandmother dear, sit by me.
Rest your eyes on mine,
Encircle me in your arms,
Hugging my soul to your loneliness.
Let your words juggle in space, Grandmother dear,
And tell me where it's hurting.
I want to see you smile like a rainbow,
And your eyes sparkle behind your glasses.
We will untie all the tight knots patiently.
Let the world outside move by quickly
While you and I are in slow-motion together.

Nan, age 28

Grandma's Proverbs

For All the Family

Remember, bad is never good until something much worse happens.

Don't take chances. You can't fall if you're on the ground.

It's not poverty if we don't have butter for our bread.

If I tell you something sinful, I'm bringing two sins on my head. One is for telling you. The other is for allowing you to listen.

Shhh! If you don't tell your secret, its your prisoner. Let it out and you're its prisoner.

If you sit on a fence, you should expect to have torn pants.

To speak kindly doesn't hurt the tongue.

If you remain silent, no one will hear you.

Listen more to the sounds of courage and less to the sounds of despair.

When nature calls, don't delay, go!

Especially for Daughters and Granddaughters

Don't let fancy phrases turn your head. There are many ways women can make fools of themselves.

Don't marry for money. It's better to have holes in your shoes.

You can catch more flies with sugar than vinegar.

Don't let your eyes wander. They give messages.

Don't be overly afraid about getting married. You're not the first woman to enter into wedlock.

Don't be afraid that a second marriage will be as bad as the first or not as good. Take a chance, but do a little sleuthing first.

A clear conscience is the softest pillow.

The best oral contraceptive is the word *no*.

If you make a mistake, turn it into a lesson.

GRANDMA'S
PROVERBS

It's not
poverty if we
don't have
butter
for our
bread

DB

11
Images and Aging: The Ultimate Discomfort

Whatever our reasons may be, many of us find it difficult to be precise about our age. It's a personal matter and our own territory. Ask us "how old" and we give an offhand answer such as, "Hmmm, I'm not exactly a teen-ager" or "I'm in the 'ish' bracket—40ish, 50ish, 60ish." When we get to 80ish or 90ish, we tell our age and brag about it.

Some of us say, "young enough," and we feel that way. Others say, "When I was a girl, and that wasn't so long ago ..." But why dwell on "long ago"?

When birthdays are under discussion, we cunningly avoid the subject. Everyone we know is at least a few months older. We never mention an exact age. Does the whole world have to know?

However, aging does give me something in common with my 6-year-old grandson. We're both losing our teeth.

Edna H.

Plain Talk

Roses, maidens and grandmothers lose their bloom. Age is kinder to some than others. We can learn to live with sags, bags, liver spots, dentures and wrinkles, or we can spend a great deal of time worrying about them.

The best face powder is still contentment and cheerfulness. Cosmetics often make us look bizarre.

Remember that when a loved one tells us gently that something in our appearance could be enhanced (they might even suggest a face lift), it's a friend telling us. We can decide for ourselves whether it's a good idea.

Trying to look younger is a waste of energy and provides dubious results. Pity the eager buck trailing the long-haired blonde only to discover she is a senior-citizen grandmother whose fore doesn't match her aft.

Many women feel aging is a cruel fate understood best by those suffering from it. In sorrowing wonder, they lament their past glories.

Some women don't suffer, however. They accept aging or work hard to slow it down and impede its abrasiveness. They often succeed remarkably well.

"It's strange," Brenda said. "My beautiful friend Doreen lost her looks completely and aged terribly. On the other hand, my homely friend Myra now looks better than she ever did. Could it be nature's way of equalizing things? It seems that beautiful women become less attractive and homely ones get better looking as they age."

The word *grandmother* used to be synonymous with age. It brought to mind images of Whistler's mother, Grandma Moses or little old ladies with gold-rimmed spectacles. All grandmothers are busy knitting, baking, sewing or polishing everything in sight.

The image of what a grandmother is has started to change, however. Now when you see two women walking together, it is sometimes hard to tell who is the mum and who is granny. They look like sisters—which may partly explain why mothers and daughters tend to get tangled up in each other's ids.

Tempus Fugit and We Fidget

Aging is a grossly unfair demolition process that goes faster as we get older. The facts are clear:

1. The only way to avoid getting old is to die young.

2. We see the effects of aging all around us in nature and in people. We should use that knowledge as an incentive to make plans.

3. We can assess what we have, then decide what we can use, what we can discard, and what goals we could try to achieve.

4. We can stop trying so hard to squeeze every bit of zest from every day. We can discover the pleasures of relaxation.

5. We can be honest about our relationships. Time contains its own anesthesia. Some friendships change and are lost. Others are characterized by extraordinary depth, kindness, generosity and understanding.

6. We can take control of our lives. This means we can gracefully bow out of unwanted obligations. We can forge our own destinies.

7. Our faces and figures may no longer be our fortunes, but our health is.

8. We can improve our health by reducing tension. We do this with smiles and soft answers.

9. Grandmothers who compete with glamour girls look like witches on a windy day.

10. Walk like a queen, and you feel like a queen. Droop and you droop alone.

11. If we talk to ourselves, we aren't necessarily crazy. Sometimes we're the only interesting people around.

12. We don't depend on others to pamper us. We promise ourselves something nice each day and try to keep that promise.

13. Weed out the shabby clothes. They've had their day, but we haven't.

14. Fat and gray will never lead eyes astray.

Trying New Responses

When someone asks, "How are you?" remember that this is a greeting, not a question. The speaker is not interested in a recital about your digestion. Try these answers instead:

"Not bad at all." (That's better than saying "terrible.")

"Real good." (You'll feel better immediately.)

"If I felt any better, I'd have to see a doctor." (This always gets a laugh.)

"I'm in good shape for the shape I'm in." (That's the spirit!)

"No complaints." (They won't believe you, but it alleviates their worries.)

"My teeth fit so well I can eat corn on the cob." (Don't overdo it!)

Better to Wear Out Than to Rust Out

KEEPING UP	OR	GIVING UP
Get going! Make plans in advance. No *ifs* or *buts.* Have something to look forward to, then do it!		**Wait and see!** Think of all the reasons for not doing anything. Why commit yourself before you know how you will feel? Listen to the weather reports.
Participate! Don't just sit there, watching exercise programs on TV. Do those exercises!		**Don't move a muscle!** Relax in a soft chair. Sip your coffee. You've earned the right to rest and watch TV.

KEEPING UP	OR	GIVING UP

Invite people over! Entertain simply and often. No need to compete as a hostess. Everyone is on some kind of diet, anyway.

Plant yourself near the telephone! Wait for invitations. Make plans for imaginary parties. It's less work than throwing one.

Be gracious! Acknowledge small attentions. When things are pleasant, say so.

Play the grande dame! Take attention for granted. Complain about neglect. Rehash faults, mistakes and callous acts of others.

Understand and forgive! Why harbor grudges, anger or resentment? We can save our strength for happy things.

Try threats! Make people feel uncomfortable, intimidated or guilty. Say something bitter or sardonic to prove to yourself that your opinions of them are justified.

Be generous! Give others the pleasure of sincere compliments and praise. Even a note shows we care.

Keep everything for yourself! Don't give presents or send notes. It's just a waste of your valuable time and resources.

12
The Winds of Change: Grandmothers Without Partners

You don't have to be a baby to cry. At any age, becoming a widow is an untimely declaration of independence.

Some of us are widowed or divorced before we become grandmothers. Grandchildren can help change our outlook, brighten our lives and fill many empty hours with contentment.

Yes, it is sad when it cannot be both Grandma *and* Grandpa. But children are grateful that they have at least one grandparent to love them. Ask anyone who never knew either grandparent.

Be glad that *you* are there. You are someone to be loved and to love in return.

When we suddenly find ourselves on our own, we look to family and friends for comfort and reassurance. They try to be helpful, but frequently they are afraid they will say the wrong thing. To be on the safe side, they tell us about the pleasure we will have from our grandchildren "who need us." We listen, but we feel drained. We are barely keeping our heads above water and our minds intact. We know that absence lasts a long, long time. We wonder whether we can begin our lives again and rediscover a zest for living.

Being on our own means learning to sleep alone, listening to the sounds of silence in the night alone, watching many dawns and recalling the sweet and the bitter. It means suffering insomnia alone, being afraid alone, crying alone, and grappling with the knowledge that no matter how many sunrises and seasons, yesterday's reality has ended. It means drifting back and wondering whatever happened to George, the boy who wanted to linger in the hallway and then shyly presented you with a gold locket engraved with a butterfly.

Being on our own means making decisions alone, fighting with service companies alone, coping with bank statements, bills, budgets, tipping alone. It means wondering who to call if the silence becomes too much and we have to reach out to another human being who understands. It means entering a restaurant and eating alone, grateful for the solid presence of chairs and tables.

Being on our own means vacant spaces in time. Ask any grand-mother without a partner whether aimless walks and hours of TV are fulfilling. She will probably say that life with her husband was better. Nevertheless, the voices of children bring us back. They are the nourishing sounds of loving and sharing. We grandmothers want little arms hugging us and a small hand holding ours trustingly. This makes us feel that it is time to begin again.

Being on our own means discovering that we have choices. We can decline, accept and extend invitations graciously. The things we've been afraid to do alone no longer seem so formidable. The day comes when we can take off by ship, plane, train or bus for a distant place. Never mind the heart's flutter and the feelings of sad-ness and anticipation as we watch ourselves embark on our new journey. We search out new faces for friends, but we do it slowly, like sipping fine brandy. And we insist upon paying for our own dinner.

Being on our own means the jarring reality of being a single woman in a world of couples. We sense the coldness in women who perceive the widow and the divorced woman as part of a cunningly constructed plot to steal her husband. Hurt wells up as invitations from the couples we know dwindle. We also feel sad and a little betrayed as we remove an insinuating hand from our knee. We try to get the message across that the single woman is not easy prey, waiting longingly in the shadows.

Sooner or later a "single" granny will decide she wants to live as fully as she can. No one has to tell her. People need human contact and companionship or they cease to grow. Good companions or friends are treasures. And sometimes they are much younger than we. Youth wants youth, yet grandmothers know that older people don't necessarily prefer the company of the elderly.

My house can be an overgrown shell, although there are times when it is my universe, my nest. Why not share it, I thought, and did just that. Knowing there is someone close, especially in the night, is terribly important to me. Living with someone can be troublesome at times, but amusing, too. One night I touched my friend Carrie's false teeth on the night table just to feel her presence.

Annabelle C.

Being on our own ultimately means discovering ways to bring out the best and the brightest in us. It means accepting the loyalty and companionship of other women and our families. We may bear a strong resemblance to what we were, even though part of us always remains private, shut off from the world and other people. But the zest for living slowly returns. We can affirm our separateness without being afraid that we are walking in a hostile world.

Alone and Managing, Thanks

There are worse things than loneliness. Bitterness is one. True solitude is beautiful and a condition for creativity. But the strength we can derive from solitude cannot be sustained if we get bogged down with resentment and feelings of deprivation.

I love the company of people who bring out the laughter in me and especially the laughter in each other. I'm not just a grandmother who wants to listen to the problems of every other person as if they are food for living. I discover that people will give sympathy for a while, but they need it for themselves, too. I love life. I love living in the midst of humanity, and it's a great thing to have three children, 13 grandchildren and six great-grandchildren. I love the fact I still play a terrific game of bridge, and that when the sun rises tomorrow, I have a good chance of seeing it.

Sonia R.

What to Do About Grandma?

Is it possible, I often wonder, to get in touch with God directly? Looking at the facts of life from the recreational lounge of the Golden Age Center, which declares nightly in neon lights, "Spend your golden years here," I don't see that many families begging grandmothers to come and live with them (not that we would accept the invitation).

My own family learned about a "service" for elderly parents. It locates apartments, takes folks grocery shopping, and introduces them to other senior citizens and ceramics teachers. It locates the nearest doctors, takes us out for walks and organizes field trips to places of local interest.

With such professional guardians, who needs family and children? At last, they have solved the problem of what to do about Grandma. At last she can be looked after properly. Her immediate needs are met and paid for. Responsibility for Grandma can be transferred with her best interests in mind.

Winnie P.

227

My daughter-in-law told me about another "service" which is more scientific. "If there is something wrong with you, Grandma," she told me, "and the doctors can't diagnose it, they can put you in a deep freeze for 50 years or more until they find the cure." "Well, my dear," I told her, "I certainly would not be interested in being defrosted after 50 years. I wouldn't know a soul. What kind of life would that be?" Mind you now, I don't suffer from a shortage of courage or imagination. This form of fastidious disposal solves lots of problems for lots of people. Personally, I wouldn't give it even cursory consideration, although it may have some mutual advantages, when you think about it. For example, it can help our grandchildren learn how they can cope with their own parents, who someday will be old and need a similar haven.

Trudy S.

Many of us enjoy the grandmother years living with our children and grandchildren. Ah, then, we must be very tactful. We can have cozy evenings alone or with them, but we can never be envious of the way they spend their evenings when we aren't there. If we're annoyed at the way the children are being handled, we can't tackle the problem like a bull in a china shop. If we suggest discipline, they interpret it as corporal punishment. We have to play it cool. If we base it on what was done when we were children, we're in trouble.

I know what to settle for. It doesn't take long to learn the fundamentals of togetherness. Once, I felt compelled to present my opinions without hesitation. Now I remain mute during a family upheaval, waiting for the moment they turn to me and ask, "Grandma, what do you think?" And that's the moment I use the shrug strategy. If I offered advice, I'd walk right into an ambush.

Hester W.

Romance and the Single Grandmother

Male companionship can be invigorating, reassuring and pleasant. We may not get an ideal paramour, but we may get a nearly ideal companion. We take joy where we find it and let it enrich us.

Even if he only talks about his dead wife's cooking, constipation, insomnia, his prostate problems or his former business partner; even if he keeps a supply of suppositories in the refrigerator and can't hear without his glasses, he can still be someone to go to movies with.

If we need someone who enjoys a visit to our kids, someone to go places with or to waltz with for a little while, it doesn't mean we have to wake up with him in the morning, prepare his cooked cereal or decide who will take out the garbage. We can afford a few small compromises here and there. Maybe he's not altogether debonair, but he may have a flair for making life interesting and for making us feel good again. He may help us get back our previous happy outlook and sense of humor. Each moment together may not fan the flames of passion, but glowing embers will do.

For some, an old eagle is better than a young sparrow. For others, however, it may be better to live with memories.

Without Benefit of Clergy

An elderly single grandmother may surprise the family when she turns up with a boyfriend in a romantic relationship.

I went on a vacation with my girlfriend, Celia, and came back with a boyfriend, Eddie, and an "arrangement." People said I looked younger and very happy. My Eddie is a real Sir Galahad. He has his apartment and I have mine. He has his Social Security and I have mine. We travel as a couple, and I insist on sharing expenses. Marriage is too complicated at our age. We both want the same thing: companionship.

To those who raise an eyebrow I say, "It depends how modern a man and woman can be, and how much openness the family can tolerate without worrying that Grandma is going to the dogs." My Eddie smiles and says, "We are making our autumn and winter years a work of art." I smile when I think of Papa. I am sure he is smiling, too. Only Celia didn't smile.

Gertrude J.

13
Yesterday, Today and Tomorrow

The years bridge yesterday and tomorrow. The generations overlap. Grandmothers look at their families with a continuing sense of wonder as little grandchildren grow up. Boundaries between the generations become blurred, which sometimes strains the spans of love. Grandmothers find their grandchildren doing some astonishing things in this fast-paced electronic age. They may not be able or even want to understand the flavor and substance of these new experiences. But they would rather be on the inside looking bewildered than on the outside looking in.

"To get 'with it' is asking me to step out of character," said Anna, a great-grandmother. "To try and keep pace would exhaust my stamina. But never underestimate a grandmother. Leave it to her and to God, who knows when a sparrow loses a feather. She'll turn up for the important occasions."

Grandmothers today are expected to be around much longer, thanks to the grace of God and the latest nutritional trends that favor longevity. Instead of looking for the right psalm for the right occasion, grandmothers are widening their field of vision. They are becoming energized by new relationships and ideas. Many grandmothers are finding new interests or exploring old ones that they didn't have time for previously. They know what they want and what they can do. They don't appreciate being pushed into action. They are comfortable doing things in their own time. On the other hand, they don't complain about their problems, either. They don't tell their families that it takes them half a day to get ready for a visit. The important thing is that they keep moving and get there on time. They know that giving in to inertia gets them nowhere.

"There's no advantage to sitting around listening to my heart perform," said Edna. "I gratefully accept invitations that get me into circulation. To be by oneself too much is not healthy. People really need people—or they stop being people."

As people get older, their emotions change. Some get more vulnerable. Perhaps grandmothers are more patient and wise with their children and grandchildren because they know anger and tension cost so much. "There is no such creature as a happy grandmother without a sense of humor," said Susan. "When I see life's patterns repeating and echoing, I have to decide whether to laugh or cry. It's so much better to be able to laugh. My mother used to say that if folks could laugh at their troubles, they would never run out of laughter. Is it just a quirk of nostalgia, or do we imagine people used to laugh together and get together more?"

Voices

When I became a grandmother, I understood my own mother as I never had before. Now she is a great-grandmother and gets maximum honors and adoration because she really deserves them. She didn't just go through the motions. She pitched right in, ready for any crisis. I look at my mother's hands; intelligent, tired hands. I look at her eyes. When they look off to one side it means she is thinking. I listen to her sing and remember how she sang to me. I also remember when she chased me around the dining-room table to give me a wallop for saying a dirty word.

Katie T.

Grandmothers should be generous with praise and things to be happy about. I know a grandmother who could be twice as mean as anyone in half the time. I told her it seems she was born with an ax in her hand. She laughed and said, "They know I don't mean any of it," but I detected a strain of regret. It's not a way to win friends in the family. Love has its own language.

Charlotte D.

My mother is a terrific grandmother. She thinks independently. She is a lawyer who never went to law school; an ambassador who never studied diplomatic relations; a doctor without a medical degree. It is her belief that conformity is an insidious disease. To avoid it in our childhood, she kept us home from school at least one day a month and told us to have a good time.

Zipporah B.

A grandmother's life is full of surprises, contradictions and remarkable consistencies. I never seem to stop learning how to deal with happiness and unhappiness. I've become the sharer of unsurpassed moments of joy, sorrow and shared secrets. Most of this has happened because I am a grandmother. I can take an affectionate look at the past.

Maria S.

Being a grandmother makes a difference. There's no question about it. There have been few greater pleasures than those which I have received from my grandchildren. I also face the fact that they don't need my daily presence and sometimes just pretend they are listening to me. When they were little, I could jabber on endlessly and sing to them. Now they say, "Grandma, MUST you?"

Ellie A.

I love to speak about my mother. I miss her and need her. She would have enjoyed being missed and needed, because she was lonely. She lived miles away from her children and grandchildren, and this was a hardship she endured for years. But she never complained. She knew I had no choice about where to live. I never told her how I longed for her closeness.

Only recently, one of my friends revealed to me that my mother "adopted" her and her children. "I was the substitute for you and your children," she said. "And indeed I was blessed."

You can't be a real daughter, mother or grandmother from a distance. Expressions of love become strained. Then, at some point, we cease tending our private gardens of life, look back and reach out.

Irena B.

My Mom had a way of saying things beautifully. "There are worse things than loneliness and illness," she told me. "One is living a small, pointless existence."

Marriage had ceased nourishing her. My father was a frosty intellectual with non-aligned emotions. His only passions were political history and physical exercise. My parents' relationship still baffles me.

My mother was a strong woman who found a way out of her parched existence. She rescued herself from emotional isolation. She enjoyed being with people and listening to them. So she managed to get my father's cooperation and opened a small private hotel. It was not a Hilton, but it had class.

The hotel was always full. Everyone who stayed there was happy. Everyone was well-fed. They could go into the kitchen any time and fix a cup of tea.

If guests were sick, my mother took care of them. It was a favorite haven for intellectuals, writers and musicians, even though many of them had little money at the time. Later, several became successful and famous. Her warmth and hospitality endeared her to those whose lives she touched. Their letters to her are collectors' items.

My mother not only survived. She triumphed.

Leona H.

I can tell you this. Parents and children can't lock one another out of their lives at any age without paying a heavy price. The sighs are audible if one or the other is not on the spot. The guilt works both ways. You can't divorce yourself from your children, no matter how old they are or how far away.

Christina D.

Memories of the Heart

With a grandmother on the scene, chances are life will be a lot more interesting. Grandmothers are the greatest bargains. We get them for nothing and the privilege of having them pays off every day. Can anyone imagine a world without grandmothers?

Grandmothers are guardians of things familiar. They are the keepers of remembrances for mothers and their children. They are the past recalled and sustained. They are the sounds and echoes of women everywhere and forever.

Grandmothers never cease remembering and reaching into the past. Some reminiscences are recalled with total clarity. Others are charming but completely inaccurate, distorted by time and the capriciousness of our thoughts and desires. For memories that live in the heart, mum's the word, and that's what grandmothers are all about.